An Obscure Order: Reflections on Cultural Mythologies

Dennis Patrick Slattery

ISBN: 978-1-950186-22-8

Cover photograph by Dennis Patrick Slattery
Cover and interior design by Jennifer Leigh Selig
(www.jenniferleighselig.com)

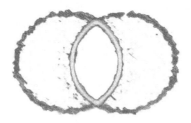

MANDORLA BOOKS
WWW.MANDORLABOOKS.COM

Dedication

To all the voices of the ancestors who have shared their wisdom with us and who encourage us to extend their work through the prism of our own imaginations.

And for Sandy, whose love and support has sustained me for over 50 years.

Reality is what forms after we filter, arrange, and prioritize those facts and marinate them in our values and traditions. Reality is personal.

~Brooke Gladstone, *The Trouble with Reality*, 2.

The personal myth is not a legend or fairy tale, but a sacred story that embodies personal truth.

~Dan P. McAdams, *The Stories We Live By: Personal Myths and the Making of the Self*, 34.

Sometimes the skin seems to be the best listener, as it prickles and thrills, say to a sound or silence; or the fantasy, the imagination.

~M.C. Richards, *Centering in Pottery, Poetry, and the Person*, 3.

Myth resembles the god Proteus in the *Odyssey,* a shape-shifting creature who knows the secret that the lost Greek sailors long to hear—the way home. But they must learn to get a grip on him, . . .

~Phil Cousineau, *Once and Future Myths*, 6.

TABLE OF CONTENTS

I
Formal Essays

II
Essays on Culture and Psyche

FOREWORD

Book titles are containers that might even precede the writing of the book itself. They are, one might say, leaps of faith into that future time when the author imagines the completion of the work that is just beginning. Within that holding place, the work is heated, cooked and simmers as the book is seasoned with spices of memory and fantasy, the herbs of dreams and reveries and, if the writer is a good cook, synchronicities and symptoms, which add that unexpected dash of flavor.

Writing, like cooking, is an alchemical art in which the title of a book, like the meal that is made, is a medium of transformation, and the alchemical art itself is a process in which the writer, like the alchemical cooks of old, are transformed.

Two questions stop me at this point:

> *Why does one ever dare to write?*
> *And is that challenge a personal, conscious choice?*

The two questions fold into each other.

One does not dare to write. That would be a most foolish thing to do, the height of hubris. One is no more the author of work that works itself through him or her, and indeed works one over in the process, than, to go back for a moment to the cooking analogy, one is the baker of the bread that bakes itself through the baker.

No! One is compelled to write, called into the work, pulled into an obligation that transforms one into an agent in service to the work.

Slattery has always been a good cook who knows how to let the bread that nourishes soul bake itself through him. He knows this in his bones.

Let's eavesdrop for a moment and lend an ear to his words about this book.

I seem to gravitate towards writing in the moment what interests me in that instant.

When I began each of these essays, I did not have a lesson plan or a template or outline of what I was going to write. But in each one there was in the beginning a shudder, a chill in me for the topic; no explanation here.

But this bodily response came in the form of "you need to write about this, or at least try."

Once, a few years ago, when I was walking with my three-year-old grandson, we stopped to look at a spider weaving its web from within its body.

Slattery's shudder begins in the depths of his being, below mind, below conscious choice or intention. The work is spun from within the flesh. In a sense, we might say that the work simmers in the blood, taking us back again to the opening analogy of book titles as containers where the work is cooked. No surprise, then, to hear what Slattery says:

Writing allows one to break something down into edible parts so one can digest it, recycle it, spiral back to it to retrieve and make of it a new experience.

So, what we have here is a book that is and is not a book. It is a book in the conventional sense of a book, with covers, chapters printed and to be published. But in its living spirit, if I may use this term, it is an invitation for dinner with Dennis.

Now, having known Dennis for about fifty years I can tell you that this meal of *An Obscure Order* is best shared along the road, as *companions* who, as author and reader, break bread together and nourish each other along the way. No upscale restaurant here. Rather, here and there a tasty morsel chosen, savored, chewed and digested.

But what to choose? When you choose from a menu whose order is obscure, the choice will reflect the habits, tastes, and preferences of the individual. So, here are some of my choices, which have fed me well.

I am sure that other readers will find their own tasty and nourishing treats. And in the end, this book that is and is not a book will continue to be cooked.

There are thirty invitations in *An Obscure Order* which bear witness to the range of Slattery's shudders and the passion of his heart. Of that thirty I was especially drawn into the conversation with Dennis by twelve of them.

Amy Freeman Lee: A Mana Personality opened the doors of memory through which she stepped into the room as elegant and spirited as when I met her almost 30 years ago. To make the past present again is the potential of memory, but it takes the skill of one whose words stir the depths before they reach the surface of mind. Then this potential of memory is a transformative moment as remembering becomes a re-membering and being re-membered.

El Dia de los Muertos: **Violence and the Opening of Consciousness** and **Moral Injury and its Healing** are conversations so apt for our time. The first one invited me to look again at the violence that has become a global issue. When it is so easy to be swept up in and swept away by its continuous presence, Slattery's shudder here re-minded me to see it within its archetypal depths. The second one did much the same, alerting me to how violence not only visibly wounds the flesh, but also invisibly scars the soul.

Photography and Painting was a delightful pause along the way. This pause, no less insightful for its delight, opened again for me the question between what Merleau-Ponty called '*etre sauvage*,' the savage being of nature's displays, and our various efforts to give expression to them. Listening to the echoes of Slattery's words, I returned to my fascination with the pointing finger, the gesture of the child that still lives in all of us, which, before any attempt to reflect, is simply responsive to the sheer presence of the world.

On Creativity: A Memoir Project and **The Power of Bearing Witness** show that the one who dares to write a memoir is the one who, bearing witness, endures and suffers a confrontation not only with what lies outside oneself, but also within. This is the deep wisdom in the art of psychotherapy and one of those places where that practice and that of the writer can converge. Writing can be therapeutic and Slattery is an exemplar of that possibility as these words from his Introduction indicate:

> *Writing is a form of spiritual contemplation, a willed openness to mystery, to the transcendent and to the personal and collective unconscious.*

My remarks above attest to six essays in Part I of *An Obscure Order* and I could do much the same for those half dozen essays in Part II that drew me into the conversation, specifically the following:

We Need the Dead in Order to Live Fully
The Truth is Hard: History May Repeal Itself
The Scapegoat Solution
A Sudden Scrape with Honesty
Conversations in a Digital Age: The Core of Civilization
When My Time Comes

But what has been said is enough now to indicate my deep appreciation for this work and to continue it by inviting the reader to join the conversation and feed soul with these nourishing gifts.

Robert Romanyshyn
Brugairolle, France,
June 2020

INTRODUCTION

Plots are myths. The basic answers to why in a story are to be discovered in myths.

~James Hillman, *Healing Fiction*, 11

All of the thirty chapter titles in this volume are concerned in some fashion and angle, oblique or straight-forward, with the nature of myth and story that Hillman's quote above gathers together. This book is my thirtieth volume. Let me clarify: I have authored, co-authored, edited and co-edited the volumes preceding this one. Two have been written but never published. I seem to gravitate towards writing in the moment what interests me in that instant; over time, they aggregate with enough volume to gather them together, as I am doing here. This may be my last collection, but who really knows?

I find that writing what interests me always has some juice to it, some energy that is psychic, physical and spiritual. I consider all writing a form of spiritual practice. I say this because there is always present in the act of writing some muse-inflected or transcendent reality that enters into the process. Some might call it the presence of one's deeper self or a Self of unknown origin. It matters less to identify it than to recognize it when it appears to guide, lead and direct my musings. These essays are musings; some of them are a-musing, but I leave that for you to decide.

All of them, however, are inflected towards a story, a narrative, or an idea with a plot line. I think that whatever I am writing about in this collection—an old friend, the death penalty, moral injury, photography and painting, creativity's hunger, a favorite writer, tyranny, conversation—I am seeking a pattern that gives that topic purpose and direction. Even when I write about an idea or a concept, I find myself in a story; ideas too have their own narrative and should not be divorced from having and enjoying a storied life. Even ideas carry or have their genesis in a myth. I like how Laurence Coupe expresses myth; he pulls from another source, the theologian Don Cupit's notion of myth's creation: ". . . mythmaking is evidently a primal and universal function of the human mind as it seeks a more-or-less unified vision of the cosmic order, the social order and the individual's life" (qtd. in *Myth* 6). So too is whatever form of expression we choose to convey our thoughts about something to others. I suggest early on that all of the thirty chapters have as their basement subject matter writing itself. Ask yourself what attracts you, what you are curious about, what you wonder about and want to explore in writing or other forms of creative expression and you will uncover dimensions of your personal myth. In another context I have explored some thoughts on writing. Here are a few of them:

- Writing is a form of discovery. Inherent in anything we wish to contemplate is an inner form that energizes and organizes the experience.
- Writing is a form of spiritual contemplation, a willed openness to mystery, to the transcendent and to the personal and collective unconscious.
- Writing is a way of bearing witness to an event, a memory, a dream, a trauma or a moment of joy wherein some formed reality seeks voice in a particular moment.
- Writing allows one to break something down into edible parts so one can digest it, recycle it, spiral back to it to retrieve and make of it a new experience.
- Writing brings shards of my personal myth into greater conscious presence and into a larger field of meaning through rhetorical midwifery. (*Riting Myth, Mythic Writing* 21)

Writing is mythic, or perhaps better said, mytho-poetic. It is a form of shape-shifting what we know into another register of awareness. When I began each of these essays, I did not have a lesson plan or a template or outline of what I was going to write. But in each one there was in the beginning a shudder, a chill in me for the topic; no explanation here. But this bodily response came in the form of "you need to write about this, or at least try." I have no doubt that each of these essays reflects something important about my personal myth. Louise DeSalvo reminds us on this point that "the key is to write in a way that links detailed description of what happened with feelings, then and now, about what happened" (*Writing as a Way of Healing* 25). Writing should be accompanied by some level of affect to be affective for the reader. I write in hopes of moving the reader to at least consider my point of view, not to agree whole cloth with it.

One of the great meditators and writers on mythology is Joseph Campbell. In one of his favorite books of mine he suggests that "the first function of mythology is to arouse in the mind a sense of awe before this situation through one of three ways of participating in it: by moving out, moving in, or effecting a correction" (*Thou Art That* 3). Campbell's sense of awe is what I call wonder; the shudder in the shoulders is the signal of awe's presence; something calls one to write about it, to explore it, perhaps because in the process something of one's own mythic life will be revealed. That is always my hope; we write ourselves further into our own identity. The "boon" that Campbell refers to as what the hero returns to the community with is the insight(s) that one comes to in journeying into and through a subject matter so it may "effect a correction" by one's additional understanding of it. That is my hope in each of these essays. Implicit in the above is the sense of how writing is vocational and vocative; it is a calling to create in words what has not yet been given a form as I understand it.

Finally, to write is to rite (right) something. Writing is a deep creative ritual that may lead far beyond what the writer is meaning or thinking. In another of my favorite Campbell books, he expresses this connection beautifully: "Mythology and the rites through which its imagery is rendered open the mind, that is to say, not only to the local social order but also to the mystery dimension of being—of nature—which is within as well as without, and thereby finally at one with itself" (*The Fight of the Wild Gander* 86). I sense that his observation also implicates a mystical sense of myth and the ritual of writing, as my context emphasizes. Writing is a back-and-forth, a spiralic motion of imagination, a curling back on itself to reconsider, revise and renew one's observations.

That has been my goal in assembling and then revising each of these essays. Each needed further face-lifting so that it would sound more right, more appropriate within itself. This last observation is not a small end point: they each gave me a sense of joy not only in the writing, but with many of them, sharing at either a conference or in newspapers as op-ed pieces. Yes, newspapers have a shelf life of a day, but in that day, there is a chance that thousands might read the op-ed essays and share them with others. That joy of sharing never grows old and remains untarnished or unsullied by repetition. I hope you enjoy these excursions into folds and pockets of our shared mythos. I cannot ask for more.

Works Cited

Campbell, Joseph. *Thou Art That: Transforming Religious Metaphor.* New World Library, 2001

---. *Flight of the Wild Gander: Explorations in the Mythological Dimension.* New World Library, 2002.

Coupe, Laurence. *Myth.* Second edition. Routledge, 1997.

DeSalvo, Louise. *Writing as a Way of Healing.* Beacon Press, 2000.

Hillman, James. *Healing Fiction.* Spring Publications, 1983.

Slattery, Dennis Patrick. *Riting Myth, Mythic Writing: Plotting Your Personal Story.* Fisher King Press, 2012.

PART I

FORMAL ESSAYS

1

AMY FREEMAN LEE: MANA PERSONALITY

In his diverse and far-reaching interests on the psyche and culture, the Swiss analyst and mythologist, C.G. Jung, was also fascinated by what he called "the mana personality." This person, he wrote, in volume 7 of his *Collected Works, Two Essays on Analytical Psychology*, carried within them "a primitive energetics" that revealed itself in any of a number of ways: as god, health, strength, fertility, magical power, influence, prestige and spirit (*CW* 7, par. 356) This person's presence was what we might call "larger than life." Jung quotes another writer in his essay, who suggests that "The Mana Personality," in his phrase is "extraordinarily potent" to describe this person of uncommon abilities, creative energetics, one who, Jung observes "is one side a being of superior wisdom, on the other a being of superior will" (*CW* 7, par. 356).

Now if we are extremely blessed in life, we may have one or two of these presences visit and even befriend us. For me, Amy Freeman Lee is one of these mana personalities, exhibited both in her formidable talents and in the expansive orbit of her interests. She was by any measure the grand dame of San Antonio, an artist, advocate of human rights and social justice, poet, board member of countless organizations, humanitarian and animal rights activist, to mention a few of her many interests. In one conversation with her she admitted to giving on average 160 talks each year both in the city and across the country. Beyond that, she was a faithful and perduring friend. I hope the following vignettes will bring Amy's abounding energy and personhood to those who did not know her.

My first real contact began when a special chair for a visiting scholar in Amy's name was introduced at the University of the Incarnate Word in San Antonio where I taught in the English Department for ten years. Amy had graduated from the institution and served on its board, becoming chair of it for many years. I was invited to be on the search committee for a national candidate who would occupy the chair for one semester. The committee would also help host the person chosen. My involvement was most prominent in the first two years. The first year, I submitted the name of Dr. Robert Romanyshyn, a former teacher as well as a nationally-known phenomenologist, cultural psychologist and poetic writer; he was subsequently chosen and launched the position. Amy loved Robert and was grateful to the committee for having selected him as the first scholar-in-residence. The second year I submitted the name of cultural critic and scholar, Morris Berman. While not as successful as Robert, Morris did introduce the faculty to the broad contours of post-modernism. During both searches Amy and I spent several breakfast meetings talking of what she envisioned a scholar should bring to the University. These meetings began in earnest our lasting friendship.

As many know, Amy's interests were vast and on-going. One could only stand by and admire her passionate involvement in animal rights, demonstrating against rodeos, promoting legal decisions on the state and national levels, her famous watercolors, her poetry, her dozens, if not hundreds of talks each year to schools, professional organizations, and several senate hearings in Washington D.C. But I most remember her finesse and leadership abilities when she invited me to be a judge for the San Antonio Poetry Project for elementary and high school students. I served with her for two years and watched as she gently but firmly moved the committee along to their choices of poems for that year. She displayed an impassioned yet impartial tone so that we never felt as if we were simply approving her choices. The discussions were heated, passionate, and of course biased towards our own choices; they were, however, not contentious, mean-spirited, nasty or brutish. Amy saw to that. I began to admire the wide range of opinions she respected but neither patronized nor pulverized.

When, after all decisions were made and we all attended the gathering of young poets at an annual award assembly she hosted, we were not only proud of our decisions, we were grateful to Amy's leadership skills and her unconditional devotion to the voices of the young to be heard on a city-wide level. At these and at all the public talks I heard her deliver, she always ended with the same words to the audience: "I am loving you." And she meant it.

Of course, she was no less dedicated to the students of Incarnate Word. I learned, for instance, that as board member and then chair of the University's board, Amy for years lived on the third floor of the Administration Building and so had a first-hand knowledge of the students, their lives, their frustrations and their accomplishments. Her choosing these living quarters so intimately within the walls of the school testified to her deep involvement with the daily life of the institution's mission. Of course, as I learned, she had an equal devotion to the Sisters of Charity, the founding order of the University, as she did to the students. She told me many times that those living quarters housed some of the best years of her life, so close was she to the vital energy of the place and the Order that she loved and served for decades.

We decided during these engagements that we liked one another, so we continued to meet: for breakfast at Le Peep and at La Madeline on Broadway in San Antonio, and at two other restaurants that were her favorites. I learned that she liked her eggs lightly poached, her toast slightly burnt, not buttered, her coffee black and her conversation keen and over not-so-easy. When we met, she always had an informal agenda of what we might entertain, but she was open to it taking its own circuitous path, as good conversations often insist on.

The topics ranged from philosophy, cultural movements, painting and art generally, the poetic imagination, politics, animal rights, teaching, aesthetics, young people, especially their enormous abilities far beyond what the culture wanted to allow them, and their reading classic works of literature in special learning facilities like The Waldorf School founded and run by Amy's close friend, Marilyn Wilhelm. What young people offered Amy, which she was nourished by, was hope. Hope she addressed often in our conversations; hope kept her balanced and secure from being swallowed by the world's violence, and worse, by the stinging atmospheres of despair and ennui.

Moreover, while she had a definite angle of vision, she wanted to know what I thought, which impressed and challenged me not to make too much of a fool of myself. An avid speaker, Amy also knew how to listen, to assess, to mull over what she heard and to respond with an originality of perspective I was always stirred by. We found, over time, an easy rhythm with one another, where we did not have to agree to have a good discussion. As a consummate learner, Amy was not afraid of entertaining and even adopting varied points of view, while never inclined to capitulate her own convictions very readily.

When I decided to leave Incarnate Word for a position in Santa Barbara, California and moved with part of my family to the West Coast, I began a correspondence with Amy that lasted over a dozen years. Look as hard as you wish, you will not find a more faithful pen pal as was she. I never wrote her without receiving within a week or ten days a response in my mail box. No emails but real letters, typed neatly on her standard stationary, signed always in a black felt-tipped pen: "Amy." Or "Love, Amy." Whether I sent her a poem, a book review, a short essay of mine, she always responded with words that revealed to me she had read and considered with careful attention what I had written.

I cannot remember when, but at one point I began to risk some of my poetry with her. What a delight to find in her letter a typed poem of her own. That began our "poetic correspondence" that continued, to the delight of each of us, for ten years. Somewhere around our house or garage, packed in shoe boxes, are letters of hers with poems in them.

One of my and Sandy, my wife's, favorites hangs in our living room, framed. It is hand printed by Amy on beautiful linen paper. It hangs just next to the front door as a reminder that Amy is a permanent guest in our home. Here is the poem as it appears:

ORIENTAL JOURNEY

MANDALAS MADE
OF STARS
WILL ORIENT
YOUR FLIGHT

AND GUARD YOU
THROUGH THE
PURPLE OF
THE NIGHT

AS GREEN
YOU GROW
THROUGH RED
GYRATIONS BRIGHT

UNTIL YOU REACH
THE WHITE OF
HEART ILLUMINATED
TRANSCENDENT LIGHT

AMY FREEMAN LEE

It has no date on it. It is all in caps in her beautiful printing. There is no punctuation. One can tell that her ear structured the poem so no punctuation was necessary. I think the poem captures her fundamentally optimistic spirit about the future, which she saw primarily in the youth of America. But she also envisioned it in an open attitude of learning itself.

Since our sons were both living in San Antonio, and our first granddaughter was there, I began an annual pilgrimage driving from the West Coast each summer to visit them. I always set up a time to meet Amy; we talked on the phone occasionally, but we both enjoyed face-to-face conversations. We would alternate between meeting at a restaurant and meeting at her Patterson Place apartment where we would be served tea or coffee and cookies or cake. Always on the menu, of course, was a rich and nutritious smorgasbord of subjects to shape and then metabolize.

These meetings were always a joy, especially so for me because I knew how busy she was. I brought with me ideas from something I was reading or teaching or writing and she, without missing a beat, would move right into the discussion with her own analogies, remembrances and insights. In spirit we found that we were closely related. Our imaginations moved often along the same grooved interests and passions without xeroxing one another's point of view.

During her last years, we visited only at Patterson. She went out less often. I was shocked one year to find, behind the immaculately-dressed and beautifully-styled hair a fading body; it showed in her face that she was ravished by disease. She did not wish to speak about it much and I did not pry. Instead, with that incisive and meditative mind, she wanted to talk about ideas, about the state of the world, about poetry and the promise she continually saw in the young. She would ask her housekeeper or me to fetch a book or painting or the like from a shelf and we would gather, as around a tribal fire, to be warmed by it and our conversation.

While her health faded, her quick wit and expansive sense of humor did not. The only time she grew quiet and revealed a wounded soul was when she would speak about betrayal of friendship and of trust. These, I know, were confidential, but the pain she felt at having been betrayed, as she understood it, made me sad. The best I could do was listen to her speak them. Perhaps that was sufficient; then we would move on to other topics. She refused to be arrested in self-pity.

The last time I saw her was at her apartment. The glow in her eyes was diminished but not extinguished; her pallor was chalky, but her voice was full of the color of a person who did not treat any single day with indifference. Her mind and heart were strong to the end of her life. The force of her soul was indomitable; no disease could touch it; no wound was deep enough to sever it. She was one of the best, most loyal and loving friends I have ever had. She was also one of the most provocative informal mentors one could wish for. But you had to keep up. Not that being with Amy was a contest, but it was a challenge, a challenge to be the best you could muster at the time. I always left her presence feeling better, more alive, than when I entered her companionship.

The San Antonio Express-News article I found quite by accident recently in a folder I kept of her death, reads: "Beloved S.A. artist, humanitarian dies." The article by Marina Pisano is dated Wednesday, July 21, 2004. Behind a glowing photo of Amy is a wall strewn with framed honors of all kinds and from a variety of disciplines. In that same folder appears a hand-written note from her: "Dennis—Hope you're "with poems"—I met James Stevens through my master teacher, Dr. Raymond Roehl—2 great Irish drinkers! Love, Amy." No date. But the poem she sent me, to which her note refers, and typed by her, explains it. The poem in the folder is entitled:

Small Perfections

(With apologies to James Stevens' "Little Things.")

The tiny red dot swirled across the printed page
Vaulting over the skyscrapers
Of the alphabet with ease
Without showing its Maltese terrier's feet

Or sharing the secret
Of its smooth sailing

Its red Volkswagen body
Interrupted by its secret Morse code
Opened its hood in the middle of its back
to create the surprise of flight;
The mechanical triumph
Is not without grace
For its winds whisper
Love songs from the past

As it continues to scurry across the page
Toward its mysterious destination
Bring no harm its way
Or you will see the invisible hand
Of St. Francis and hear the roar
Of Zeus' thunderbolts,
But let it touch my hand
So that I might feel
The nature of perfection

Amy Freeman Lee
San Antonio, Texas
May 30, 2004—12 noon

By the date in which she typed it, she had only weeks to live, but that was no concern of hers; the poem was. And only Amy would put "12-noon," so precise was she as artist and poet. Finding the poem now, in December, 2009, is her early Christmas gift to my family and me. And speaking of automobiles. . . .

I can still see her, in earlier years and in better health, pulling up at La Madeline restaurant on Broadway Ave. in that enormous Town Car she loved to drive. Such a big car; out of it would emerge this immaculately dressed prim woman carrying within her the wealth of ages, ready to share it with you if you were ready, so inclined, and up for the challenge. I said to her at the end of our last breakfast out: "Let me buy." Her response: "No, I've got this one." And doesn't she now?!

Work Cited

Jung, C.G. *Two Essays on Analytical Psychology*, vol. 7. *The Collected Works of C.G. Jung*. Edited by Sir Herbert Read, Michael Fordham, et.al., translated by R.F.C Hull. Princeton UP, 1953/1966. pp. 227-41.

2

MYTH, FILM AND CULTURE: A TRIUNE UNITY*

If we are simply satisfied by repeating and reporting C.G. Jung's thoughts, pronouncements and musings, then nothing is truly engaged, no movement occurs and our thinking Jungian can slowly devolve into a cult-like rehearsal. Jung himself would rather we take in his words, assimilate them with our own thinking, and then create out of the crucible of our imagination a new form of thought, some new angles of envisioning what he evoked in us. We study Jung by making him our own; we each create our own Jung, as we each create our own *Odyssey*, our own *Divine Comedy*, our own *Moby-Dick*. To do any less would be to slow down the momentum of new ways of knowing based on what we have assimilated. The psyche needs renewal to flourish; without that stimulation, it languishes.

I have been asked to speak on the above Trinity of forms, as I want to call them. Alchemically, I refer to them as vessels, holding tanks, reservoirs of both influence and confluence. But I am biased, so I want to suggest that myth is the primary vessel that holds us, film, and culture in compatible company. If I were to set them in size as various Russian Matryoshka dolls, then myth would be the big mother, inside of which would be culture, and within it would be film as the smallest figure. Each of them, however, offers in their own formative being a way of knowing, of comprehending and dreaming their content

* Delivered at the conference, "Salubungan on Depth Psychology: Our Psyche, Our Earth" at Club Filipino, San Juan Metro Manila, Philippines on July 6th, 2016.

forward. Each also carries their own ontology, that is, their own beingness, or metaphysical reality in its narrative as it continues on its journey of becoming.

What they share--and there may be many formats for responding to this assertion—is a desire, an Eros, to make something present through affect. By that I mean that they do not want to be simply an idea in the head but an embodied felt experience that touches the heart. So, myth, film and culture each establishes its own metaphor of the real. Each wishes to give a formative shape, as artifact, to experience. For each is involved in an on-going creative making or shaping reality into lived experiences, a kind of *poiesis* of the soul, wherein *poiesis* is understood as a shaping or a making of something into a form that can be contacted and shared by others.

In fact, when a critical mass of a population accepts the constellated metaphor that touches the heart of their complex, as a formidable and persuasive view of reality, then this agreed-upon metaphor becomes the shared sense of what is true about the world. That culture's religious view is no exception. Such is the process by which myths are formed, crafted and dispersed through the imagination of a people; in its formation it outlines the Zeitgeist, or spirit of that age in history.

Here is Jung in his Introduction to *Psychology and Alchemy* as he addresses the nature and function of religion:

> The history of religion in its widest sense (including therefore mythology, folklore and primitive psychology) is a treasure-house of archetypal forms from which the doctor can draw helpful parallels and enlightening comparisons for the purpose of calming and clarifying a consciousness that is all-at-sea. It is absolutely necessary to supply these fantastic images that rise up so strange and threatening before the mind's eye with some kind of context in order to make them more intelligible. Experience has shown that the best way to do this is by means of comparative mythological material. (1968/1970 *CW* 12, par. 39).

I do not believe Jung would argue if we were to add that strange and fantastic images also rise up out of the darkness of the movie theater in film and that they too often carry rich mythic images within the context of a plot that corresponds in some measure to our own storied history. Listen to him compare the theater to the movies early on in *Dream Analysis: Notes of the Seminar Given in 1928-30* (1938/1984), a volume I strongly recommend to you all. Compared to film, Jung finds live theater wanting: "The theater is the place of unreal life. It is life in the form of images, a psychotherapeutic institute where complexes are staged; one can see how these things work. The movies are far more efficient than the theatre; they are less restricted, they are able to produce amazing symbols to show the collective unconscious, *since their methods of presentation are so unlimited*" (1984, p. 12, italics added).

In another volume he directly addresses the efficacy of a particular film to render a complex idea: that of God born as a man who then must "suffer the terrible torture of having to endure the world in all its reality. This is the cross he has to bear, and he himself is a cross" (1958/1977 *CW* 11, par. 265). He then finds the best analogy, of which more will be said shortly, in a film he enjoyed watching: "These thoughts are expressed with touching simplicity and beauty in the Negro film, *The Green Pastures*" (par. 266). Jung's praise of this film is motivated by how well it revealed God ruling "the world with curses, thunder, lightning and floods," but to no avail. Only then he realized he would have to become a man himself in order to get at the root of the trouble (par. 265).

Christopher Hauke's fine essay, "Much Begins Amusingly and Leads into the Dark: Jung's Popular Cinema and the Other" published in *Jung and Film II* (2011) leads us back to a scene in *The Red Book* where Jung has a conversation about the cinema. Before revealing the scene, Hauke offers as prelude Jung's earlier questioning "his own impulse to reject popular mass entertainment like cinema, and has an epiphany in realizing its human significance and value" (2011, p. 112). Then to *The Red Book* scene: Jung is traveling in the country when a coarse-looking man, scar-faced and with only one eye, joins him. The man relates to Jung he is not happy working for a farmer, so he now wanders looking for other work. He and Jung fall into conversation; the man complains that in living on farms and with their people, there is "no stimulation, the farmers are clods" (2009, p. 265). Jung's response is one of astonishment; what does this man really seek? He asks him: "what kind of stimulation is there in the city?" To which his scruffy companion responds: "You can go to the cinema in the evenings. That's great and it's cheap. You get to see everything that happens in the world" (2009, p. 265).

Now Jung's reflection on his fellow traveler's excitement about the cinema is curious: "I have to think of hell where there are also cinemas for those who despised this institution on earth and did not go there because everyone else found it to their taste" (2009, p. 265). After which he asks the man traveling with him:

> I: "What interested you most about the cinema?"

> He: "One sees all sorts of stunning feats. There was one man who ran up houses. Another carried his head under his arm. Another even stood in the middle of fire and wasn't burnt. Yes, it's really remarkable, what people can do" (2009, p. 265). At first Jung seems to dismiss this man's idea of mental stimulation; but then, placing the image of the man carrying his head, as well as the other two images his companion offers, into a historical religious context, he changes his mind about cinema's value. Now, "I regard my companion with feeling—he lives the history of the world—and I?" (2009, p. 265).

We should not miss as well a passing observation of Jung's in *Civilization in Transition* in his chapter, "The Spiritual Problem of Modern Man" where he addresses the current "spirit of the times, about which everyone has so much to say because it is so clearly apparent to us all" (1964, par. 195). This spirit, he goes on to name,

> shows itself in the ideal of internationalism and super nationalism . . . we see it also in sport and, significantly, in cinema and jazz. These are characteristic symptoms of our time, which has extended the humanistic ideal even to the body. . . . This tendency is emphasized still further in modern dancing. The cinema, like the detective story, enables us to experience without danger to ourselves all the excitements, passions, and fantasies which have to be repressed in a humanistic age. It is not difficult to see how

these symptoms link up with our psychological situation. The fascination of the psyche brings about a new self-appraisal, a reassessment of our fundamental human nature (1964, par. 195).

Jung continues noting how the body itself may be rediscovered through the media mentioned above, which unfastens a discussion of how film's invention is on one level, an attempt, often successful it seems, to rediscover the body "after its long subjection to the spirit— we are even tempted to say that the flesh is getting its own back" (1965, par. 195). I do not have time to work this discovery out, but it is a rich moment in history for human embodiment's retrieval through the "motion" picture. Film, then, is psyche's invention, both cultural and mythic, to retrieve the body and to set it before us as a film, or screen, to reconnect us to our own enfleshed reality.

Cinema as well provides an inroad into cultural history; it also offers a corridor into myth, or better, said, mythopoiesis—a shaping or founding images into creative forms. So, let's at this juncture connect film to mythos.

I recall mythologist Joseph Campbell's assertion that new myths call up new art forms to give them expression. Film, I sense, creates a tension between objective and subjective realities, between fantasy images and historical illustrations. What draws film and myth into a more intimate relationship is captured in a word that I believe lies deep in the bones of Jung's thought on analogy, a word which I want to add to our Jungian lexicon, but which originated with the Greeks: Mimesis.

Mimesis rests on the capacity for imitation. We see our word "imitation" as well as "mime" and "mimic" in its folds. Aristotle informs us in the first literary theory work in the West, his *Poetics*, that to imitate is a natural response in us that gives pleasure (336 BCE, p. 11). Watch a child play, or engage him or her in play. A child will engage imitation and repetition for extended periods of time because imitating and repeating that imitation gives her pleasure, even joy. It is a basic life nourisher and enhancer. It also rests at the heart of our desire to play. Friedrich Nietzsche reminds us that "In every real man a child is hidden who wants to play" (qtd. in Klein, 2012, p. 35). Later in life we realize that something deeper is at work in mimesis. Aristotle tells us that it is "an imitation of an action" (336 BCE, p. 95), a story that resonates invisibly in the soul of the audience as a consequence of the plot's action on us. I would frame it this way: the plot of a story relates to its deeper action in the same manner that the myth of a person or a nation relates to its affective meaning. Affective because it must carry an emotional energy or charge to be felt as important and meaning-full. Fundamentally it is libidinal energy.

Here is how cultural historian Stephen Halliwell speaks of mimesis in relation to the Socratic dialogue, *The Timaeus*. "Mimesis is a key to the structure of the world and of reality, which is to be comprehended in terms of correspondences and interrelations between mimetic subjects and objects" (1987, p. 118). He furthers his argument by noting that mimesis suggests "everything created is a correspondence to what is invisible, a higher order or paradigm of existence" (1987, p. 117). Thus, the motion of psycho-poetics includes a synthesis or a constellation of the visible and invisible realms that narratives have the capacity to unite to make our lives' past events into formed and coherent experiences that integrate these two realities; one is more attuned to the facts of our past, the other to the mythopoetic truth of our histories (Slattery, 2014, p. 107).

The nature of story-crafting, including the stories that myth and film offer as expressive mirrors or imitations of a culture's deepest beliefs, includes a persuasive narrative structure that creates a likeness, an "as-if" quality to assist us in regaining a rightful place within an archetypal constant whose power is so great as to be able to reorder one's life. Stories, then, heard, read or seen in a theater, are akin to what Joseph Campbell calls metaphors—that is, they serve as "transport vehicles" (that assist us in reentering the archetypal space that Jung points us to repeatedly). He is clear that "Metaphors only seem to describe the outer world of time and place. Their real universe is the spiritual realm of the inner life. The Kingdom of God is within you" (Campbell, 2001, p. 7). My own sense is that this re-ordering or re-organizing principle is the substance of myth.

Finally, on the subject of mimesis, for it lies so centrally in the imagination of Jung and his sensibility about psyche, is this notion of Aristotle's. In his study of the *Poetics,* critic O.B. Hardison reminds us that in addition to imitation, poetry itself also carries its delight to us as readers through both harmony and rhythm. He further observes that "Aristotle refers to the fact that imitative works, if they are well-crafted, reveal generic qualities: the presence of the universal in the particular, and that the spectator or audience learns from this (336

BCE/1968, p. 93). Now what he calls "universal" seems analogous to what Jung refers to as the archetypal realm of psyche, which gains its greatest persuasive force through its particularities, not its generalities. Furthermore, "imitation would seem to contain a calculus of inspiration; by means of it, some amount of curative energy is released to bring one back into right relationship through an imaginal knowing, by way of the power of narrative presence" (Slattery, 2014, p. 107)

So just before I turn to Jung's deeper understanding of myth, a word on the relation of metaphor, analogy and mimesis. I link this series of words because I believe they comprise the basic heartbeat of depth psychology. Mimesis, as an imaginative representation, introduces, even evokes, the power of the analogical, the way in which consciousness discovers analogies of its experiences in other forms of narrative. I mention this connection because of the Neo-Platonist, Plotinus, who was a major influence on both Jung and James Hillman. In his *Enneads* he makes the observation that "all learning takes place by likeness" (1992, p. 40).

To pin this sense of analogy, on which mimesis rests, a bit more, I ask you to consider this dependent adverbial clause of Jung's in volume 9, 2, *Aion: Researches into the Phenomenology of the Self.* I believe it largely defines the core of depth psychology. Remarkably, Jung tucks it into a dependent clause: "Since analogy formation is a law which to a large extent governs the life of the psyche. . . ." (1959/1970, par. 414), and I skip the independent clause that follows because we don't need it. We might recall that what brought Jung around to seeing the value of cinema earlier is that he found rich analogies from religious history to connect with what his traveling companion witnessed in cinemas— fantastic images that nonetheless had historical precedents.

Jung's assertion above, that "analogy formation is a law" of the psyche, that this capacity, this miracle of the imagination to create likenesses, simulacra, representations, metaphors—and may I add here, symbols?—of experience so to see doubly, to grasp something again, but on a different register of consciousness, is the fundamental bedrock of imaginative engagement with the world. The act of interpretation, by extension, then might be understood as an act of inter-penetration, of a mutual mating of self and world. The bridge that connects them will depend on the tensile strength of the analogy as well as its power to affect presence, as a poetic expression.

Just to step back for a moment. I am suggesting that film and myth are both forms of narrative expression that rest on the power of the analogical. Film is a relatively new form of a successful transport vehicle which seeks to create in us as audience an emotional landscape, a geography of affect, through an air of imaginal credibility but perhaps only if I can suspend my disbelief and cultivate a complete submission to its "moving" narrative logic. Filmic images carry forceful psychic energy to place us, preferably in a dark theater of the unconscious, somewhere between, for a span of a couple of hours, body and spirit, between inside and outside realities, which you may recognize in the language, a fragile *mundus imaginalis*, in the words of Sufi scholar Henri Corbin. He distinguishes between two worlds of apprehension that is crucial for this presentation: "Of course, the forms and figures of the *mundus imaginalis* do not subsist in the same manner as the empirical realities of the physical world, otherwise anyone would have the right to perceive them" (1964/1972, p. 8). In addition, I hazard that excellent and enduring films carry us into something like a waking dream state, which beckons the culture into a dreamscape so that it can envision itself anew.

On the order of a dream, film can rise to the status of a symbol-carrier, as Jung, in speaking of a flying saucer dream, calls the UFO a symbol carrier (*CW* 10, par. 706): "the UFO appears to be rather like an exemplification or 'projection' of the symbol. The dream insists on the projection character of the UFO, since it proved to be a cinematographic operation conducted by two rival film producers" (par. 706). Of course, we don't miss the play on "projection" here, analogous to the images of a film projected from some invisible room behind us to the blank screen before us, reminding us of Plato's rich "Allegory of the Cave" imagery in his *Republic*. The white wall of the show space receives the simulacra of images that can affect us more than our daily round of waking images are allowed or invited to do.

I will devote the remainder of this presentation to exploring Jung's sense of myth and relate it to film and culture. We recognize the powerful alchemical vessels these three terrains offer us for further exploration in themselves and in confluence with one another.

I recommend to you the fine series entitled *Encountering Jung: Jung on Synchronicity, Jung on Death and Immorality, Jung on Mythology, Jung on Active Imagination,* and *Jung on Alchemy,* to name a few. They are superbly edited and each contains an introductory essay that dramatically sets the context for the passages from the *Collected Works* that follow. The strength of these books is that you are reading Jung, not someone telling you how to read Jung or how that editor read Jung. At this stage of the game, only the original sources should be our goal.

The editor of *Jung On Mythology,* Robert Segal, an excellent mythologist in his own right, offers: "Because the collective unconscious is inherently unconscious, it can communicate with consciousness only indirectly, through intermediaries like myth" (p. 85). I begin here because I want to sustain an active through-line regarding analogy, mimesis, metaphor and mythology. I also ask us to consider how all three of my arenas in this presentation—myth, film, and culture, are in effect intermediaries of our experiences, helping, each in its turn, to form, shape and give sustained meaning to our lives. "Myth," Segal, continues, "is a good intermediary when the conscious literal meaning of a myth suggests another symbolic meaning, which for Jung, is the most psychological one" (1998, p. 84).

The term "suggests" puts us back into the mimetic mode, which is the mode of analogy. It also suggests the fundamental connotative disposition of psyche, which, not coincidentally, echoes one of Joseph Campbell's major theses on myth: Myths offer, he affirms, a rich series of connotations in a world grown fiercely denotative, that is, full of single meanings. "All of our religious ideas are metaphorical of a mystery. It is vital to recall that if you mistake the denotation of the metaphor for its connotation, you completely lose the message that is contained in the symbol" (2001, p. 48). It may also be the dehydrated source of literalism, fundamentalism, indeed all closed circuits of beliefs and interpretations. By contrast, according to Jung, "myths and fairy tales give expression to unconscious processes and their retelling causes these processes to come alive again and be recollected, thereby reestablishing the connection between conscious and unconscious" (Segal, 1998, p. 88). Do we not hear in his exploration the broad outlines of the transcendent function, which is activated by myth and story, by myth *as* story, and film as story? James Hillman will return to the term *reversion* to capture something of Jung's *recollection* (Hillman, 1975, pp. 30 ff).

Have each of us not experienced a film for the first time or read a story for the first time or watched a dramatic performance, and suddenly felt that we were in the act of remembering something from our past? We are suddenly activated by a memory that shaped us earlier and now, here it is, analogically expressed in a new form that is simultaneously remembered in our own original form. Such is the shaping property of mimesis, analogy and mythopoesis that this essay is intent on giving a fuller expression to.

Jung furthers this last observation when he muses on the nature and function of an archetype: "archetypes create myths, religions and philosophical ideas that influence and set their stamp on whole nations and epochs" (Segal, 1998, p. 95). We could add here that a work of fiction, and here I am thinking of classical works of poetry, is comprised of a deep reservoir that comes directly out of the cultural psyche. "Myths of a religious nature," believes Jung, "can be understood as a sort of mental therapy for the sufferings of mankind, in the form of hunger and wars" (p. 95). He concludes that "the narration or ritual repetition of sacred texts and ceremonies . . . grip the audience with numinous emotions" (Segal, p. 96). I suggest that analogy's energy enters the imagination not simply to inform but to transform the soul, to set right an attitude that cripples, to free one from restraints of a narrow set of beliefs, through the power of the poem's capacity to be present affectively.

One of my favorite volumes of the *Collected Works* is *The Spirit in Man, Art and Literature*. Sadly here, Jung does not include film, but I must, for certain films, and I leave you to name your own, can and do reach the level of artistic visionary creation. Like works of literature, which Jung divides into psychological and visionary in his essay, "Psychology and Literature," films too can be so categorized. In psychological works of literature and film, the work is already done: "Considered as a self-contained whole, such a novel explains itself. It has done its own work of psychological interpretation. . . (*CW* 15, par. 136). There is little else to say about it. It is like a baked loaf just out of the oven. Its work is done.

But a visionary work of fiction—which as I said I am including film as aesthetic fictional expression of something much more complex and even numinous—transports us somewhere else. Visionary fiction requires a deeper imagination from the artist to produce and the audience to fathom. Jung's language to describe visionary fiction is too delicious to paraphrase: "But the primordial experiences rend from top to bottom the curtain upon which is painted the picture of an ordered world, and allow a glimpse into the unfathomable abyss of the unborn and of things yet to be. Is it a vision of other worlds, or of the darkness of the spirit, or of the primal beginnings of the human psyche? We cannot say that it is any or none of these" (*CW* 15, par. 141). We are left, Jung believes, in this experience confused and disordered; "we demand commentaries and explanations. We are reminded of nothing of everyday life, but rather of dreams, night-time fears, and the dark, uncanny recesses of the human mind" (par. 142).

I applaud his language and his insights here, for he chews right through the notion that art, literature, film, and other forms of creative expression are shaped to make us comfortable or to simply entertain and distract us as "escapes," when in fact the opposite, it seems to me, is more valid: art should perturb, unsettle, make one uncomfortable, knock one out of one's bubble where we keep things arranged and safe, free of uncertainty or questions about existence both personal and collective. I suggest that this effect is the vocation of myth as well.

Myths, for Jung, represent typical psychic phenomena; their crucial import for this discussion is that they "reveal the nature of the soul" (Segal, 1998, p. 70). The poet, then, including here the filmmaker as poet, as one who shapes the myth into a coherent form, crafts the myth, giving it aesthetic shape and organic form; the upshot of this creation is that it becomes something deeply remembered. In fact, Jung suggests in another context that any study of the collective unconscious—that reservoir or vessel or container of inherited images common to us all—happens best through mythology and through analysis of the individual. I would add a third: through mythopoesis. Keeping the vial or vessel intact increases its content's viability through its contained vitality or energy. One's individual psyche is such a vessel, film as culture's vessel, myth as a people's vessel and culture as that vessel which holds the myth intact; all of these containers hold the primal material for the study of depth and archetypal psychology. In my understanding, the most vital reason for such a study is to retrieve or renew or rediscover the richness of living a symbolic life, one where a polytheistic understanding rather than the tyranny of monotheism holds sway and informs one's general awareness.

If such an imagination were to be adopted, then fundamentalist stances toward global warming, extinction of species, exhaustion of the earth and of ourselves, could gain a reprieve and open to other avenues of redeeming what little is left for us to negotiate in resources and in the psychic health of the planet. Psychic salvation could begin through respecting the earth's limitations and reclaiming a gentler use of her rich gifts. Fundamentalisms leave no gap in their absolute posture; depth psychology's study promises gaps, which could make our relation to the planet a bit more gappy, by restoring a mythic imagination to the discussion, for there much of our origins reside. With gaps, our thinking has a better chance of being flexible, a bit wiggly, loose and adaptable in solid correspondence with the reality that gives us coherence. Without these open spaces to reconsider and entertain new ways of thinking of Gaia's psyche, we are doomed to exhaust her and ourselves in our non-reflective rush to devour what sustains us. May it be otherwise! We can each contribute to such a reclamation.

Acknowledgement: I am grateful to Joji Racelis, Vice President of the Carl Jung Circle Center in Manilla, for creating the PowerPoint images that accompanied my presentation.

References

Aristotle. (336BCE/1968) *Aristotle's poetics*. (Leon Golden, Trans.). Commentary O.B. Hardison, Jr. Englewood Cliffs, New Jersey: Prentice-Hall.

Campbell, J. (2001). *Thou art that: Transforming religious metaphor*. Novato: New World Library.

Corbin, H. (1972). Mundus imaginalis: Or the imaginary and the imaginal. *Spring: An Annual of Archetypal Psychology and Jungian Thought*. New York: Spring Publications, 1972. 2-19.

Halliwell, S (2006). *The poetics of Aristotle: Translation and commentary*. Chapel Hill: University of North Carolina Press.

Hillman, J. (1975) *Revisioning psychology*. New York: Harper Perennial.

Jung, C.G. (1938/1984). *Dream analysis: Notes of the seminar given in 1928-1930)*. (William McGuire, Ed.). Bollingen Series XCIX. Princeton: Princeton University Press.

Jung, C.G. (1953/1968*). The collected works of C.G. Jung*. Vol. 12. *Psychology and alchemy*. (G. Adler & R.F.C. Hull, Eds. & Trans.). Princeton, NJ: Princeton University Press.

Jung, C.G. (1957/1964*). The collected works of C.G. Jung.* Vol. 10. *Civilization in transition* (G. Adler & R.F.C Hull, Eds. & Trans.). Princeton, NJ: Princeton University Press.

Jung, C.G. (1959/1970). *The collected works of C.G. Jung.* Vol. 9, ii. *Aion: Researches into the phenomenology of the self* (G. Adler & R.F.C Hull, Eds. & Trans.). Princeton: Princeton University Press.

Jung, C.G. (1966). *The collected works of C.G. Jung.* Vol. 15. *The spirit in man, art and literature* (G. Adler & R.F.C Hull, Eds. &Trans.). Princeton: Princeton University Press.

Jung, C.G. (2009). *The red book: Liber novus.* (Sonu Shamdasani, Ed). (Mark Kybruz, John Peck and Sonu Shamdasani, Trans.). New York: W.W. Norton and Company. Philemon Series of the Philemon Foundation.

Jung, C.G. (1958/1977). *The collected works of C. G. Jung.* Vol. 11. *Psychology and religion: West and east.* 2nd. Edition. (Sir Herbert Read, Michael Fordham, et. al., Eds). Princeton: Princeton University Press.

Hauke, C. and L. Hockley, eds. (2011). *Jung and film II: The return. Further post-Jungian takes on the moving image.* Routledge.

Jung, C.G. (1998) *Jung on mythology.* (Robert Segal, Ed.) Princeton: Princeton University Press.

Klein, D. (2012). *Travels with epicurus: A journey to a Greek island in search of a fulfilled life.* New York: Penguin Books.

Plotinus. (1992). *The enneads.* (Stephen McKenna, Trans.). Burdett, NY: Larson Publications.

Slattery, D. (2014). Mimesis, neurology and the aesthetics of presence. *Creases in culture: Essays towards a poetics of depth.* Skiatook, OK: Fisher King Press.

3

El Dia de los Muertos: Violence and the Opening of Consciousness[*]

True, whoever looks into the mirror of the water will see first of all his own face. Whoever goes to himself risks a confrontation with himself.

~C.G. Jung, "Archetypes and the Collective Unconscious," par. 43

Allow me to begin with a story, a story about a violent man and a violent deed that reverberated across the planet as a particularly horrendous act, but one that fits far too painfully into a series of violent acts that seem to characterize something deep within our own culture. This essay hones in on this one act in order to try to grasp what myth may underlie this historical event and others like it. Here is the story that shapes the event in retrospect.

I had been invited by the Unitarian Universalists of New Braunfels, Texas, where I live, to participate in their celebration of *El Dia de Los Muertos* on Sunday morning, November 5th 2017. I was to speak on "Our Necessary Relation to the Dead: A Memorial Tribute" because the Sunday service was devoted to remembering those members they had lost during the past year. Service would begin at 10:30 a.m. and I was to speak at 11:00. I had addressed their

---

[*] Presented to the Mythological Studies Program at Pacifica Graduate Institute, Carpinteria, California, March 20, 2019.

congregation several times before and always enjoyed being invited back.

In the front of the church was an elegant altar with many candles burning, flowers in vases, and photos of many of those who had died since January 1, 2017. After songs by the congregation, followed by several from the church choir, and a fairy tale told to the children who had gathered by the altar to listen, I was invited to the podium.

I began by first reading a poem entitled "Obituaries" by the former poet laureate of the United States, Billy Collins. I had been asked beforehand to limit my talk to between 20 and 25 minutes. I looked at the clock on the back wall as I began. It was 12:00; it had not been turned back an hour from the night before, so it was 11:00 exactly and I contoured my talk to finish at 11:25, which I did. Of course we could not know at this moment until later in the day, that five minutes after I finished my presentation on the living and the dead, and just 38 miles southeast of the church in which I spoke, a young man from New Braunfels, Devin Patrick Kelley, began his rampage slaughtering twenty-six of the parishioners of The First Baptist Church of Sutherland Springs, Texas with a semi-automatic rifle.

The horror of his actions was increased by what I and the congregation of the church I spoke at had just witnessed in remembrance: the passing of their own members. The events of that day, which could not be immediately absorbed by any of us, was too big and too traumatic to be comprehended, and in our surroundings we all became aware of the eerie coincidence that was to have lasting effects on us as it quickly grew into an international story.

On Monday, the day after the massacre, I discovered quite by accident the Farm-to-Market road in New Braunfels where Kelley's parents' house was and where their son had been living; I felt a compulsion to drive at least into its vicinity for reasons that were unclear at the time and remain so at this writing. As I came around a bend in the road, I saw police cars parked in a short driveway leading up to an iron gate that marked the Kelley house, which was not visible from the road. One cruiser had all his lights flashing; across the street were two camera crews waiting for whatever or whoever might show up. I felt such a sickening feeling in my stomach, as well as an onrush of fear, that I turned around and drove the 15 miles back to our home in the same city.

Many reasons for Kelley's violent behavior were put forward by several sources, motives which I will not enumerate here. But I thought every day of the members of First Baptist Church, prayed for them, donated money to their needs, then reached a psychological and emotional threshold on the morning of Friday, November 10th that surprised me. I decided in that moment to cross it and drive the 50 miles southeast from my home to Sutherland Springs.

As I came into the small set of stores that comprise this quiet and peaceful town on Route 87, I saw immediately along the side of the road close to the church and a large tent being constructed for church services on November 19th, a long thick row of flowers, balloons and crosses with one name painted on each. Next to every one of them were letters to the dead, notes from family members and friends, all clustered along the highway; these tributes and expressions of love and loss extended around the corner leading to the church property. I had parked my Harley-Davidson motorcycle across the street at a Valero service station, which I later learned was where Kelley had also parked his car and where he was initially spotted before the shootings. He was described as dressed all in black—a dead man walking—just before he unleashed his fury on the members of the congregation a short distance across the street.

I walked around to the front of the church and was surprised to find it open; a row of cars on each side of the street attested to the number who were there at the same time I was and with the same intention: to visit the place of the massacre that occurred less than a week earlier, and to extend their condolences in any way possible. For many, it was as well to express their grief over the loss of family and friends. A sign instructed all who entered not to take any photos inside the church. Everyone obliged and kept their cell phones out of sight. I signed the guest book and then stepped into a space of great peace and purity.

Inside, all the walls, floor and ceiling had been scrubbed and painted white, actually a brilliant white. White wooden chairs were placed in various spots from the church's front to the back door, each decorated with a name written in a bright color; a rose was taped vertically on each chair. The spacing and position of the chairs signified where each parishioner who had died was seated at the moment of their murder. In the front was a Bible under glass and a note behind it stating: "Psalm 100 was scheduled to be read to the congregation that morning." It never was because of the violent invasion that entered the door before the Psalm had a chance to be read aloud to those who came to worship. Here is the Psalm we can read together now:

Psalm 100: A Psalm of Thanksgiving

Make a joyful shout to the
Lord, all you lands!
Serve the Lord with gladness;
Come before His presence
with singing.
Know that the Lord, He is
God:
It is He who has made us, and
not we ourselves;
We are His people and the
sheep of the pasture.
Enter His gates with
Thanksgiving,
And into His courts with
praise.
Be thankful to Him, and bless
His name.
For the Lord is good;
His mercy is everlasting,
And his truth *endures* to all
Generations. (*The King James Version,* 689)

A sound system carried the recorded words of a man speaking throughout the church, of the joys of peace and love. People moved around the inside of the hall quietly and with great reverence. The site had become a magnificent and potent shrine in which to pray and remember the dead and the wounded—indeed the entire community of Sutherland Springs in their grief and mourning. I could not help but feel the heartache and the love that permeated this small white church and its members; some of them mixed with us as well as those who drove here to witness the aftermath both of the violence and the redemption one felt within its pure white space and on its grounds.

Many of us simply stood by one of the walls and reflected on what had occurred so recently. I sensed that others like myself prayed for some understanding of what had happened. The violent act by one lone shooter was for me, surrounded by a potent sense of mystery, of unfathomability. Such is violence's power when it is unleashed under any circumstances. The circumstances of this outrage made it more mysterious, not less.

When I left, reluctantly, I noticed and walked up close to twenty-six small crosses woven into the chain link fence surrounding the grounds. Each had the first name and first initial of the last name of each of those who died so unexpectedly that morning only days ago. Three flags ruffled at half-mast in the church's front yard. The sun was bright in a fall Texas sky, its brilliance matched only by the white-washed interior of the church.

Now I do not want to speak about gun control or the "why" question that haunts these more frequent abruptions of violence in our nation and now, locally and less than an hour's drive from my home. I wonder far more about the mystery of violence, even the myth of violence—for it carries its own powerful psychic energy—and of where it rests in the soul, heart and mind of individuals, tribes and nations. What this experience pushed me toward was meditating once again, at the very site of the killing of twenty-six parishioners, that included the fourteen-year-old daughter of the congregation's minister, several other children and a woman pregnant with her own developing child, as well as those who were in the hospital struggling to survive. I was led to contemplate the nature of violence itself, not the one who was violent. These concerns may not have possible or even satisfying descriptions or explanations. But I sensed, as I have before, that several concerns which may not be able to be answered even now, with incidents of violence nationally continuing to stockpile in our collective soul, are still worth reflecting on. I believe that violence, like other archetypal conditions or situations, has its own autonomy and voice. C.G. Jung might well refer to it as an "archetype of transformation" (*CW* 9, 1, par. 80). That presence evoked in me a series of questions as weak attempts to grip the nature of this impulse in the soul:

- What is it that the voice of violence wishes to say?
- What does violence in all its forms, want from us?

- Who or what is speaking through violence? Rage? Insult? Impotence? Recognition? Woundedness? Frustration? Feelings of exile? Hunger for community?
- What is it that may have been displaced, even orphaned, abandoned, deserted and is now seeking a home and is searching, granted, in a destructive way, for its own resonance as well as its own resolution?
- Is violence a grotesque form of a rite of passage, even a response to a feeling of social and spiritual exile?
- What is the archetypal ground of violence, its original *arche,* its defining principle, that points to its reality in the soul of an individual, a tribe or a nation? ("The Voice of Violence" 213)

Certainly it is a human urge to recoil in horror at these events that we should resist accepting as an old familiar pattern or "new normal" in our society. But seeking a single cause in an individual or group avoids the deeper question of violence's multiple voices in our society in so many outbursts of exasperation. What more profound mystery inheres in violence that we have not yet excavated, but rather seem to be mired in asking "why" and then seeking a cause/effect answer in the individual's or group's past? "Because" answers do not go deep enough, in part because they skate across the surface of explanation, not deeper through the aperture of meditation. Here I draw the distinction that C.G. Jung makes in the beginning section of *The Red Book,* "The Way of What is to Come."

There he reveals two spirits, the spirit of the times and the spirit of the depths (*The Red Book* 119). The former's interest, which highlights "use and value," understands phenomena through the prism of history. It seems a more horizontal disposition of understanding. But the latter is both beyond and deeper than the former; it has been with us "from time immemorial and for all the future possesses a greater power than the spirit of this time" and has succeeded in stripping from Jung his belief in science and "forced me down to the last and simplest things" (120). This push into depths put him "at the service of the inexplicable and the paradoxical" which cultivates "the melting together of sense and nonsense, which produces the supreme meaning" (120). Such a revelation also stimulated in Jung an abiding and lasting interest in mythology, which rests so often on an acceptance of paradox. Perhaps then, Jung offers us a roadmap for understanding such a powerful archetype as violence, as I hope to illustrate below.

I also want to engage voices who have expressed insights into the nature of violence in order to tempt the discussion away from cause-effect reductions, which seem to me closer to an imagination of the spirit of the times. In his chapter, "Killings," psychologist Wolfgang Giegerich traces violent murders back to the origins of consciousness itself; he insists we consider this, for some, horrifying question: is coming into consciousness itself a violent act? ("Killings" 201, 204) Does it require violent behavior, an overt transgression, witnessed for example in its formative stages in Aeschylus' *Prometheus Bound,* Shakespeare's *Hamlet* or Fyodor Dostoevsky's *Crime and Punishment*— indeed in the movement of tragedy as the literary genre of violence? What are the connecting ligaments of violence to consciousness and to the sacred, if Giegerich and René Girard (*Violence and the Sacred*), among others, are correct in their respective assessments? I can also not help but think of the Christian mysteries of the agony in the Garden of Gethsemane, the crucifixion and resurrection. They are contrary mysteries, and violence seems to have had a major, if not an essential role, in directing the resurrection to fruition.

It seems that in at least a number of historical events, we cannot separate violence from sacrifice, which for Giegerich is the most pervasive phenomenon in an overwhelming number of world civilizations ("Killings" 194-98). I wonder then: when the fundamental experience of the sacred is the sacrificial killing, then in our time, and as the event at the First Baptist Church above seems to indicate, the fundamental experience of the secular, the profane, the gratuitous killing, or the violent action itself, absent the necessary boundary of ritual to contain it, to keep it vesseled, explodes with uncanny force all around us.

The failure of our cultural conversation to discern these acts of uncontained and boundless violence does not want to be faced. I believe it is because in part, it does not recognize or seek the psychic or mythic ground behind such actions, the terrain of the spirit of the depths, the arena of myth's cultivation, wherein deformation and affliction are two additional conditions that inform both archetypal psychology and poetics. For James Hillman, "Imagination becomes a method for investigating and comprehending psychopathology"

(*Archetypal Psychology* 51). How strange it is to our ears to think about the questions: how are we to imagine violence? Its voice? Its plea? What may *it* desperately need from *us*? Yet these and other like-minded wonderings open us to "the spirit of the depths" (*The Red Book* 119), which for Jung nudges one along the path of individuation, of becoming the whole self that one is destined to be.

We have witnessed far too many violent acts of murder wherein the killer, at the end of a paroxysm of vicious acts, turns on himself and, we are told, commits suicide. But is it? Can it not also be a form of self-sacrifice? Perhaps we have been misconstruing what takes place here as suicide when, in fact, from the angle of a more mythic reading, it is self-sacrifice, that is, a completion of the sacrificial killing where consciousness itself is struggling, however futilely at times, to awaken. Is this where the sacrificing of others leads? When aborted, incomplete or unfulfilling, it may be precisely because it lacks the sacred or mythic character of the ritual killings mentioned earlier because it is divorced or orphaned from any sacred context and because all boundaries and containers have long since been rejected and ejected. Is it this recognition of the horror of the act, divorced from a larger context, that brings the hand of the murderer to self-sacrifice? Might it be the fear of punishment and persecution? Of course, it need not be either/or.

In earlier times, as Giegerich develops this idea of violence, human killing was less concerned with biology and nature as it was with soul and mind, which he claims, grows from those original necessities of psychology and spirit (200-02). Hunting was itself a crucial ritual, a "sacred action occurring in a sacred space" (201). Today, I would think that violence is enacted as a vague simulacrum, a paler mimetic secular representation of this original sacred behavior. Then he offers what I find to be an amazing proposition: "Through killing man gained his initial self-knowledge, his first awareness of himself" (205-06). Killing as separation of the human from the animal order was its primary objective and its ultimate intention.

The pivot between immediate natural life of living creatures and cultural existence of mortals was "posited and mediated with a blow of the axe on the animal" (212). He hit and killed his own Other, thus himself. In this act of violence towards animals, Giegerich believes, the soul was born as *Homo sapiens* and then shifted from gatherer to hunter, inaugurating a qualitative breakthrough into a new dimension: the mind and soul of consciousness itself. I have to ask here in this complex mix of motives and mythic presences, if achieving consciousness itself through violence is a paradoxical human endeavor because it at once, by analogy, slays oneself, which is a necessity for a liberated, informed and aware form of consciousness to be born? Is violent killing at once a human birthing? It seems that it might reveal one of the deepest paradoxes of being human: that the death of something/someone is the birth of something/someone at the same instant.

If it is true that the soul first made itself conscious through killing, then is there a way of speaking of violence today, desperate and unpredictable, because the larger sacred ritual has left it—a larger numinous story to guide it and give it some achieved form of containment? Thus, violent acts today are ghastly in a culture with little historical consciousness of the place of violence; we are left to wonder in the void: Why? And we are far too ready to affix the appellation SENSELESS to these acts. What a fix this set of thoughts puts us in. We deny the existence of the very thing or force that feeds the complex, inciting the archetypal energy, and most dangerously, rupturing the container that we wish to address and make fool-proof.

The eruption of violence today, as well as its acceleration into deeper forms of the grotesque, serve as reminders—memories even—of this split and dismissal of the violent acts that brought consciousness into being, as Giegerich asserts (203). In order to protect the innocence of consciousness, he presumes, psychology has taken up only the symbolic and metaphorical sides of the human person and left the historical-biological act of violence back there, unkempt, polluted and exiled to the miasma of history (203). The historicity of body consciousness has been relegated to the back burner of the cultural stove. Consciousness has indeed been stoved. His claim is that we have dismissed the violent acts that brought consciousness into being: "The archetypes are immunized from the actual world's relation to an age and culture" (206), in large measure because they have lost their memory of the literal events that brought them into being—acts of violence. Perhaps we should think of Giegerich as an archetypal literalist.

More to the point, Joseph Campbell helps us here in his observation that to break from the exclusive fetters of biology is to enter mythology, which he took great pains to tell us, originates in biology (*Flight of the Wild Gander* 27-41). There he attests that "symbolism, the protection of the psyche, is no less necessary than the nourishment of the soma" (35). We might venture here that the development of myth lies somewhere between these inner and outer realms at least as much as it involves some coherent vision for ourselves between the microcosm of our bodily being, the mesocosm of society, and the macrocosm of the larger created order.

Perhaps then the way to a deeper understanding of violence's voice and veracity in culture is to reunite the literal with the symbolic, the historical with the metaphorical and poetic, and to imagine them from a double-visioned point of view, a double seeing that may allow to emerge the paradox inherent in violent acts.

As I drove the 50 miles home, I thought of the church exhibiting a paradoxical presence not just to me but to all those who came on their own pilgrimage to this site. The paradox was that at once this site of prayer and violence, sacred and secular, faith and fierce emotions, was able to contain both. But only by being bodily present in this space, a sacred site of violence and forgiveness, of a quiet acceptance of what had occurred so recently living side-by-side. At some point one grows out of attempting to explain such human horrific behavior and moves into another space, as I began to in memory when driving home. I passed the side street in New Braunfels down which the Unitarian church I spoke at less than a week before rested quietly. A church just like this one, with a modest but devoted congregation, who gathered each Sunday for worship.

I could not help but compare the two houses of worship and the authentic, sincere and beautiful way each addressed their God. Accepting violence's place in the world is difficult and exhausting with each incident like this one that abrupts suddenly into our midst to question, challenge and hold up for meditation what we assume about our individual lives and their mingling with those of others. I felt, as I pulled into our driveway, a peace descend on me and pervade my thoughts. I knew that this short pilgrimage to the site of horrific destruction had its match in the love and humility, the quiet peace and strength of First Baptist Church's congregation that was shared with each of us who ventured into its white-washed enclosure to be healed of our own internal conflicts. I believe that this is what an act of grace imparts to any who seek it.

Works Cited

Campbell, Joseph. "Bios and Mythos." *Flight of the Wild Gander: Explorations in the Mythological Dimension.* New World Library, 2002, pp. 27-42.

Giegerich, Wolfgang. "Killings." *In Soul-Violence: Collected English Papers. Vol. Three.* Spring Journal Books, 2008, pp. 189-266.

Hillman, James. *Archetypal Psychology.* Uniform Edition 1. Spring Publications, 2004.

Jung. C.G. The Archetypes and the Collective Unconscious. Vol. 9i. *The Collected Works of C.G. Jung.* Sir Herbert Read, Michael Fordham, et.al, editors, translated by R.F.C. Hull. Princeton UP, 1971, pp. 3-41.

---. *The Red Book. Liber Novus. A Reader's Edition.* Edited by Sonu Shamdasani. Translated by Mark Kyburz, John Peck, et. al. Philemon Series. Norton, 2009.

Slattery, Dennis Patrick. "The Voice of Violence: Its Afflicted Utterance." *Harvesting Darkness: Essays on Literature, Myth, Film and Culture.* iUniverse, 2006, pp. 205-225.

The Holy Bible. King James' Version. Peabody, MA: Hendrickson Publishers, Inc., 2006.

For Further Reading

Armstrong, Karen. *Fields of Blood: Religion and the History of Violence.* Alfred A. Knopf, 2014.

Bailie, Gil. *Violence Unveiled: Humanity at the Crossroads.* Crossroad Publications, 1997.

Bok, Sissela. *Mayhem: Violence as Public Entertainment.* Addison-Wesley, 1998.

De Vries, Hent and Samuel Weber, eds. *Violence, Identity, and Self-Determination.* Stanford UP, 1997.

Diamond, Stephen A. *Anger, Madness, and the Daimonic: The Psychological Genesis of Violence, Evil and Creativity.* SUNY P, 1996.

Dostoevsky, Fyodor. *Crime and Punishment.* Edited by Jesse Coulson, translated by George Gibian. W.W. Norton, 1964.

Ehrenreich, Barbara. *Blood Rites: Origins and History of the Passions of War.* Henry Holt, 1997.

Gilligan, James. *Violence: Reflections on a National Epidemic.* Vintage, 1997.

Girard, René. *Violence and the Sacred.* Translated by Patrick Gregory. Johns Hopkins UP, 1997.

Grossman, Lieutenant Colonel Dave. *On Killing: The Psychological Cost of Learning to Kill in War and Society.* Back Bay Books, 2009.

Maalouf, Amin. *In the Name of Identity: Violence and the Need to Belong.* Translated by Barbara Bay. Penguin Books, 2000.

Selzer, Mark. *Serial Killers: Death and Life in America's Wounded Culture.* Routledge, 1998.

Slattery, Dennis Patrick. *The Wounded Body: Remembering the Markings of Flesh.* SUNY P., 2000.

Strong, Marilee. *A Bright Red Scream: Self-Mutilation and the Language of Pain.* Viking, 1998.

Whitmer, Barbara. *The Violence Mythos.* SUNY P, 1997.

Young, Dudley. *Origins of the Sacred: The Ecstasies of Love and War.* Harper, 1992.

4

MORAL INJURY AND
ITS HEALING*

Some years ago, I became fascinated with the place and power of wounding, dismembering, tattooing, body markings as well as illness in a cluster of literary classics in which bodily wounding, dismembering, patterning, scarring and tattooing were the main characters in the drama of the flesh. I wished to explore what the body wounded and distorted in various attitudes told us about the psyche, about the emotional life of the individual as well as the forms of expressions they exhibited within that wound through the aperture of the poetic imagination. I wished to entertain that being embodied is not a condition alone, or a physical construction. It is also a place, a situation, a locale, the origin of opportunities for an emotional, spiritual and psychological life, and finally, for personal transformation.

I wrote many years ago how I wished to explore the body as it is changed, deformed, incarcerated, fatigued, bludgeoned, decomposed, made into something else by the world—where the world marks it. And I would ask: Is being wounded a gift? Is there a gift imbedded in the wound? For me, the gifts are two prosthetic hips that I had inserted over a span of twenty years; one of them required wounding me more than once, both to install and to replace because of a serious bacterial infection that attacked the prosthesis—all of which took wounding me to install. Now I walk freely without a limp and without the chronic

---

* Presented to The Jung Society of Austin, Texas, November 30, 2018.

pain that had successfully kidnapped my life. So too was it true when I underwent an emergency appendectomy; my life was saved because of fast-acting doctors and surgeons.

Is being wounded, then, I asked, a way of inhabiting the world in a new way, such that what was conventional was no longer sufficient? The wound is a special place, a magical locale, even a numinous site, an opening or aperture where the self and the world may meet on new terms, perhaps violently, so that we are marked out and off, a territory assigned to us that is new, and which forever shifts our tracing in the world. . . . Serial killers are part of its lexicon that needs closer examination to show body and world as a piece, or as mirrors of one another (*The Wounded Body* 7).

I also considered back then that "to be wounded is to be opened to the world; it is to be pushed off the straight, fixed and predictable path of certainty and thrown into ambiguity, or onto the circuitous path, and into the darker depths of what is unseen and unforeseen. One begins to wobble in life, to wander, and perhaps even to wonder not only about one's present condition, but also about one's origins. Circling the edges or the lips of the wounds we carry, so to speak, one's vision may clear, one's perception sharpens, and one may grasp for the first time what James Hillman describes in *The Soul's Code* as that "innate image" that lies at the heart of the acorn that is me (qtd. in *The Wounded Body* 4), that defines my heritage and my destiny. How one lives one's embodiment out, especially in its hyperbole—its exaggeration in woundedness—reveals the acorn's possibilities as well as its origins. It is to see the form of one's life at once, without development, without linearity, and without theory. It is to grasp the form of one's being in an instant (*The Wounded Body* 13-14) through a perception mediated only by the affliction or the infection itself. Being wounded offers us a new way of seeing; something is exposed to the light of psychic and emotional life that invites the sacred into its precinct, its domain, its bunker. Being wounded is territorial, both terrible and insighting.

But now I am interested in pursuing the wound further. Yes, we can be *mortally* wounded, but we can also be *morally* wounded, as Larry Kent Graham observes in his book, *Moral Injury: Restoring Wounded Souls*. Other writers have also expressed growing interest in this sphere of being. Where the body is wounded, afflicted, infected and *inflected* by illness, so also can the soul be morally wounded, needing healing every bit as much as any physical assault on us or by us, for we are of course capable of both. Before I take up Graham's explorations of *Moral Injury,* however, I want to explore the pioneering work of psychologist and mythologist Edward Tick with American veterans of war and the traumas of combat as a preface to affirming the power of moral injuries. Then to the main thrust of this presentation on Graham's equally cutting-edge exploration of the ways we find ourselves paralyzed in life by moral dissonance, moral distress as well as his search for ways to aid those in often debilitating circumstances.

But first, I want to be forthright about what has driven me to consider what moral injuries are and why they are crucial to recall, name, reframe and revise, if not actually redeem from the corrosive place of their habitation. Some of the language I just used is from Graham's *Moral Injury* book. For the past two years, since the Trump presidency has been in place, I have felt assaulted by the president's outrageous behavior that I believe has been tearing apart some of the most cherished institutions, qualities and values of our country. (Now, as I revise this essay, it is almost four years since his inauguration and we are suffering through a pandemic as well as a debilitating virus of denial that emanates from the Oval Office.)

I found myself assaulted by new insults to reason, to fair play, to those who are on the margins, including myself, as well as the violent rhetoric he spews and the lies he propagates without flinching or ever admitting that what he said one day has been proven false just hours or days later. I am not asking you to agree with me; I want, however, to recover the major influence on me to pursue this contagious and psychically life-threatening realm of moral injury. Like a pandemic, it too can devour or liquidate all connections to the shared reality most of us contend with daily.

I also found myself angry at his incompetence, of his reveling in his own ignorance and his lack of desire or felt need to learn about the office he now holds as of this writing and prior to the midterm elections. I felt the wounds of outrage stacking up in me, like a cord of wood, ready to catch fire, as well as the moral outrage over a Senate that remains largely silent, and therefore complicit in his words and actions as the rampage on decency and on the traditions of our country are plowed under, out of sight. I also felt the growing number of injuries suffered by so many by the conscious stoking of foreign agents, reinforced from within our country, of divisiveness that continues to turn our citizenry against one another through the virus of hate and fierce tribalism and by the fierce pandemic of incompetence.

I found myself regularly yelling back at the television screen during a range of reporting or in the presence of the president's slanders and mean-spirited invectives tossed out to impress a crowd of acolytes hungry for such spittle; the moral injury gathered in me from what I felt was misleading, downright deceitful and continually wounding to the nation as a whole, regardless of one's party loyalty. I began to ask what was happening to me such that I found little peace during the day as I carried around in my emotional backpack stories, reports, speeches, and violent attacks on others that demeaned the presidency and all of us nationally, whatever our political or ideological leanings. I felt bruised as a constant condition and dismembered when the rhetoric accelerated and intensified. I recognized that I was also the culprit in my self-wounding when I allowed myself to be sucked into the field of influence, an influenza field, a vortex of violence and betrayal of human decency. I felt in constant need of triage.

I write these words not too distant from the midterm elections rather than waiting to hear what and how they may change my and others' perspectives. So, this presentation is dated, although I commented above that its revision was almost four years into Trump's term in office. It is written at a particular moment in history and is open to revision and editing as events unfold. Further, and to my surprise when I returned to one of my more recent books, *Riting Myth, Mythic Writing: Plotting Your Personal Story*, that on a couple of chapters on wounding, I had already been giving voice to the deep emotional, psychological and spiritual wounds we can self-inflict, have inflicted on us *by* others, or that we have more than a modest capacity to inflict *on* others. I have since discovered how Ed Tick, Jonathan Shay and Larry Graham have helped me deepen my appreciation of this malady infecting modern politics. I hope to bring part of this work as well as those of Graham and Tick, into our retreat tomorrow.

But first to Ed Tick's work, specifically in *Warrior's Return: Restoring the Soul After War* that follows his earlier work, *War and the Soul*. My intention here is to pull from his 300-page study some illustrations of the soul wounded. He senses from working with veterans for decades, many of whom he returns with during an annual pilgrimage to Vietnam, that healing will only happen when they come home to where the wounding began to reclaim their soul they left in Southeast Asia as many as 40 years previously. War and its trauma, Tick believes, separated them from their soul life; their moral injury grew from such a traumatic soul separation and encouraged such a distressing divorce. So, Tick relabels the trauma from Post-Traumatic Stress Disorder, which he senses trivializes the wound, to Post-Traumatic Soul Division, a far worse malady than a more innocuous, by comparison, stress-related suffering. He calls it thus because of his understanding that it is a moral trauma, not only a psychological condition (17).

He furthers this discussion by suggesting that PTSD can be suffered by a nation's soul (36) as well, and has the capacity to sterilize a culture, making its moral immune system easily exposed and overrun. I believe that my earlier description of my own rage and feelings of insult because of the current poisonous political climate has the toxic energy to bring such a condition on to many, to say nothing of our grief over our many military involved in wars in multiple locales, most especially in the exhausting two decades in Afghanistan. I believe we all carry that conflict deep in our own unconscious and are affected by it daily, even as it squirms beneath the floorboards of consciousness. I would include the Vietnam War in that same category. Interesting too is the fact that the Vietnamese people call that same brutal conflict "The American War."

While I am on the subject of our wars currently in production, Tick mentions in his study that since the founding of our nation, we have NOT been at war with someone for a total of twelve years. He also clearly points out how "many veterans are in anguish over the ways—hostile, demeaning, neglectful, political, patriotic, or gratuitous—they were greeted upon return. They seem destined to carry the traumatizing consequences of being dishonored back to the country that was so willing and encouraging, even eager, to send them there. One young Iraq veteran he hones in on was refused a VA disability rating, benefits or help. In early 2011 he left a suicide message that declared, "'Maybe they'll finally see my invisible wound when they stare at my flag-draped coffin'" (125). The moral dissonance this young veteran felt is repeated countless times with others who served well but were not recognized as doing so by their treatment when they returned to the powers and the people that sent them there. Homecoming for so many was itself a deep war wounding; returning to the site of the conflict was, by contrast, often healing and restorative.

Far from incidentally, the figure of 22 veterans committing suicide in the United States daily has been a constant for several years now; what a further moral injury it is that they are not recognized or acknowledged as casualties of the war they faced at home when they sought services or other forms of help from a system that they entered voluntarily with a desire to serve us. Theirs is a deep soul wound that many cannot cope with, in part because of how it can shatter their sense of who they are and why they originally served their country. Being honored, Tick points out repeatedly, is a form of healing, both for the population and its leaders who instigated the war, as well as for the vets themselves.

The invisible wound, Tick argues, is itself an identity crisis (145). Here is one of the most crucial qualities of moral injuries: they have the power to dismantle us, to flatten our resolve to heal or to reclaim our past life prior to war's horrors and to diminish us in the eyes of others. Pushed closer to the edge, they can destroy the Eros even to live. Tick offers this image: "trauma stamps dinosaur footprints into our psyche and the pre-war self cannot be recovered. This constitutes a psychospiritual death. A new self must be constructed that includes the important stories, values, and meanings of military and war experiences. . . . The invisible wound is an identity crisis" (145).

I have used Ed Tick's work with veterans to highlight the power of moral injuries; now I will introduce Graham's *Moral Injury: Restoring Wounded Souls* and work with it for the remainder of this presentation. I am also interested in following his outline for dealing with such injuries to introduce how writing may be a useful way to give voice and name to our moral injuries, especially through Louise DeSalvo's excellent study, *Writing as a Way of Healing*, which I find so valuable in giving some level of coherent shape to our moral afflictions. I would mention here as well the fine study by Edward Whitmont, *The Alchemy of Healing*, where early on he observes that to simply "vest the sickness [or the moral injury I add] with dignity is to vest it with a healing power" (37).

Graham lays out his process of working with moral injuries through a number of categories. But first to the nature of moral injuries, which on one level are understood to be a "failure to live in accord with our deepest moral aspirations" (11). *Moral,* and we can work this term to include more, is "a sense of right, fairness in obligations that I feel in events of my everyday life. *Moral* includes our core values, our virtues held by my communities about what constitutes the best way of life (12). This definition is very close to what mythologist Joseph Campbell has called a myth; a myth places us in accord with our inner selves in relation to the outer world we negotiate daily. Mythic dissociation, his term, occurs when we become discordant with our myth or with the myth we are enmeshed in socially, politically and spiritually. He writes specifically that the kind of religious thinking that divorces God from daily life brings about a "'mythic dissociation.' The sense of an experience of the sacred is dissociated from life, from nature, from the world. . ." (*Flight of the Wild Gander* 167).

Graham terms this condition "moral dissonance" wherein I recognize that my internal sense of right/wrong is unclear or in conflict with my life presently. Moral dissonance, however, is not just about interior conflicts; it can arise from a moral climate in which history and culture have embedded/embodied us. "The moral climate is a matrix of operative moral values and demands that arise from our interacting moral environments which place obligations upon me and my communities" (13). Such moral codes "are connected to our families, cultures, religions, nation, ethnicity, gender, race, economics, professional lives and politics. They are both hidden and transparent, synchronous and dissonant, liberating and oppressing" (13). We cannot help, as Graham believes, "but to live in such multiple moral landscapes, . . . which is the source of pervasive moral dissonance in our personal and social lives" (13).

Reading these ideas, I felt, as I mentioned at the top of this presentation, how dissonant are the Trump invectives, attacks, belittlements, lies, deceits and self-serving Narcissism to my own values, and that he and his regime pretend to represent me, when clearly there is no trace of that in his words or in his efforts to dismantle policies that seemed to be based on common sense and not self-serving goals to benefit the few as he demeans and tries to erase the good done by his predecessor.

When we become ensnared in a moral dilemma, which Graham suggests "arises when we find ourselves required to choose or act against one's moral good at the expense of another value we hold" (13), we cannot escape such a dilemma when it comes into play; we must respond. "What we do may advance us morally or lead to moral injury or moral demise" (13). Here he approaches Ed Tick's thinking earlier when Graham equates moral injury with moral trauma, which can drain us of our vitality, shake us from previous values and identities and send our moral compass spinning in circles. He labels moral compass as "the internalized organization of our moral identity (ethics, values, and moral codes)" (14). I would add that these and other elements comprise what I call our personal myth, our own unique identity in the world, both shaped by history and culture as well as innate in us as a core essence of our soul lives.

Moral injury ensues when our lives and the lives of our social groups diverge from what we believe to be the best in ourselves, or when our moral actions lead to a diminishment of value for self and others. Compassion wanes in such an atmosphere where conflict flourishes. But I can also be morally injured when I find myself violated by others who may wish to impair my moral sensibilities about right and wrong (*Moral Injury* 13). I would ask at this juncture: where in your life do you feel most morally injured, vulnerable, and perhaps feel a desire to avenge another or others, or to flip the tables and forgive? This question and others in accord with it are well worth giving form and shape to. When, for example, have we set out and achieved injuring another, only to realize that the deeper wound was inflicted on ourselves, such that we became or become the recipient of our worst and most active impulses to harm?

When I ask this question I suddenly remember how my father's fierce shame and guilt accrued from his alcoholism, which he used in part to camouflage his own suffering, and was with uncanny expertise passed on to the five of us children so that we carried not only our own feelings of inadequacies growing up in a violent household every weekend, but his as well. Our backpacks were filled to burdensome overflowing. We all learned that moral injuries can be passed down through generations; we continue to live out the darkest corners of a parent's myth. I sense that a deep moral injury can be the consequence of having trust questioned or toppled from our lives because of myriad examples of violence. We look into our respective backpacks decades later and are not really astonished at how much of it is filled with the heavy weight of shame and rage.

Graham then focuses on what is involved in healing from such injuries that includes: renewal, repair and reconciliation, each of which contributes to reframe suffering as a soul wound/injury. His next observation seems crucial to this entire topic. He tells the story of how a therapist "reported that though her clients appreciate the language of PTSD and the language of current mental health treatment modes, 'when the language and concepts of *soul wound* or *soul injury* are introduced, a place of substantial identity arises to consciousness in a profoundly tangible way'" (15). He goes on to report that "when they 'reframe' their suffering as a soul wound/injury, that deep inexplicable place in them of humanness becomes valid" (15). The consequence of such a recognition is a validation of a client's ability to "reclaim the experience of that deepest part of themselves and work on healing the wound" (15). The naming or renaming of the wound as a soul injury helps one to feel their own humanness in a new way; naming it as a soul wound is already an act of reclamation. Contrarily, and returning us to a moment at the beginning of this essay, demeaning, trivializing and deceitful language from our political leaders and commentators moves us in another direction; we feel the moral sting, if not puncture, to ourselves when others are maligned, made less human, or more monstrous through language's power to invent realities that may have little accord or authentic traffic with the truth.

To say it another way, we place our experiences into categories in order to give them a fuller, more coherent context to our lives. In my book, *Riting Myth, Mythic Writing: Plotting Your Personal Story,* I suggest that a personal myth "organizes my experiences of the world and determines or influences by what categories I will engage the world's matter." I continue this line of thought by adding that a personal myth "molds my life events according to categories of awareness" (19), to which I would add in a revision: "and to categories of bewareness," namely, to those places that we may be most vulnerable to and prefer to beware letting material in that would threaten these soft, tender, raw pockets in ourselves. Myth is reality-shaping and framing. Jung called this "as-if" quality of the soul a way of creating metaphors that can be so persuasive in what we accept or reject as true of our experiences and the world at large. He points out that every "archetypal content expresses itself first and foremost in metaphors" (*CW* 9, 1, par. 267).

The linguist George Lakoff reminds us in his very influential *Don't Think of an Elephant: Know Your Values and Frame the Debate,* which has been recently revised and expanded, that the frame you set content into is as potent as any material you place in it: "Frames are mental structures that shape the way we see the world. . . . You can't see or hear frames. They are part of what cognitive scientists call 'cognitive unconscious'—structures in our brains that we cannot consciously access" (*Elephant* xv). Framing an idea, an image, a point of view, a prejudice will have enormous rhetorical, persuasive as well as pervasive power in convincing others of its veracity. Reframing can also be an effective rhetorical template of consciousness. It seems to me that myths, both personal and collective, are also frames, i.e., ways of seeing or attitudes of seeing and believing. Yes, an attitude is a frame. How frequently we can be framed by our attitudes!

Graham suggests that to reframe our conversation about moral injury and moral healing, it is necessary "to mainstream our moral discourse, share our moral feelings and flaws in a realistic and nurturing public context; only then will there emerge a greater chance of repair, of integration and understanding so to slow or stop the momentum of the injuries levelled at us personally and collectively with the destructive potential of a pandemic virus. His motto to collapse the dichotomy and animosity between ourselves and others is to reframe our commonality; he uses the phrase "I Am as We Are." He borrows this shorter version of a phrase from one of two non-Western sources that he calls on throughout the book, both African philosophy and Native American perspectives (20). His short phrase grows from an earlier African religious one: "I am because we are and since we are, therefore I am" (21). His sense here is that we can then ask the honest questions: Where are our values? Inside me? Out there? Between us? The phrase just mentioned that inspires these questions is itself based on a myth that highlights the community over the individual.

In addition, the Native American perspective that Graham uses to work on moral injury, moral dissonance and healing includes the idea that "to be human is to be comprised at all times by all our relations" (21). None are left out or sidelined or trivialized. If we were to take a moment to create a list of all the varied kinds of relations we are each involved in daily, we would be surprised; they are gesturing in the background of who we are all the time; I am, as an example, in relation as grandfather, father, husband, teacher, writer, emailer, painter, presenter, facilitator, friend, homeowner, health client, to name a few. Each of these categories places me in relation to a host of others. Often only when a rupture occurs in one of them does it step forward and need added, if not more focused, attention and compassionate care.

Both non-Western traditions he leans on in his methodology rest on the solid ground of the following belief: "Problem solving emerges from the interaction, not what is formulated from outside or above and then imposed on participants" (24). "Palaver" is the name for the process he uses, which was developed by a Native American student, Tapiwa Mucherera. It is a word with several meanings, but the one highlighted is a conversation or colloquy between different peoples of many levels of a society. Its focus is the following: honestly naming the problem; reevaluating the interpretative schemata maintaining the problem; exploring the negative consequences of the problem; and reformulating new understandings and practices for addressing the problem (24). All levels of participants have a voice in the discussion but none alone determines the outcome (24).

Graham uses the term "contextual creativity" to describe this method of palavering or engaging a communal conversation. He uses the phrase as a synonym for "human freedom, agency, autonomy, and self-realization. It is the basis for dignity and resistance in the face of evil . . . as well as for imagining and creating new configurations of personal and social life. He uses the example of Martin Luther King's "I Have a Dream" speech as a flagship insignia of this method. Courage is needed in all participants in order to realize the success of this method and more importantly, to move towards a consensus of a possible healing of our "moral narratives" from a morally dissonant condition suffered individually or collectively. Contextual creativity, he continues later, adds to furthering its understanding: Contextual creativity is a capacity to receive with appreciation the concrete circumstances that make up the dissonances/dilemmas we actually face, and to imaginatively respond with creative alterations that accept life as in flux; we can shape what life will be through our engagement with dilemmas, destructive thoughts and urges and dissonance that distances us from others that confront us (55).

Polarizing, chastising, demonizing, scapegoating, demeaning—all work against contextual creativity's abiding interest in finding within differences and dichotomies the courage and will to remain civil and respectful of others' angles of vision. All forms of us/them, right/wrong end stop the possibility of creative palavering. The large task today, Graham believes, is to mitigate warring moral orientations that threaten our welfare and continue to inflict moral injury on one another. Strife seeks separation; conversation cultivates community, even when differences are apparent.

Here follows a few examples that stimulate morally injury in me: I feel morally injured when I learn of the myriad ways that voter suppression is being furthered and cultivated nationally; efforts to keep minorities from voting, changing voting places; excluding any ballot where the name is slightly different from the voter registration, then singling out those with the least power or pockets of votes who have traditionally voted in favor of one party; rigging voting machines to break down, then changing voters' choices when they come back on line; deceitfully trying to keep college students from voting where they are attending school in another city or state that is different from their home.

Graham offers this example in his book: He tells the story of a minister, 63-year-old Pastor Gregory, who engages a prisoner who commands the prison population. In their conversation, Gregory persuades this prisoner to change his grip on power for a moment to pardon one prisoner who has violated a protocol the lead prisoner has initiated, and who will be punished severely. Gregory gives the leader of the prison, a prisoner himself, a chance to choose mercy. He agrees (63). He learns from his action that he has gained a freedom that the prison cannot take from him.

Another example from *Moral Injury:* Mrs. V. is suffering on life support. The medical team overseeing her condition wants to disconnect her and allow her to die. Family members, however, insist that she continue to live artificially on the equipment. Mrs. V. has been a practicing Buddhist for many years and is faithful to her yoga meditation. One day both the family and the medical team gather around her bed. Her son speaks to her; she smiles and holds his hand. The medical staff changes its diagnosis and allows her to go home to live with her family (65-66).

The nature of moral injury is not always about one's own moral failures and flaws; they can arise from the moral stance of others. Graham illustrates with additional examples wherein individuals sustained moral injuries at the hands of others. One Methodist minister, a black woman, came into conflict with her church elders over something she believed strongly in. But neither side would budge from their viewpoints. Graham writes that her actions "were dissonant with theirs; our moral actions can put us in harm's way to be injured.

Personal injury can be the result of acting out of our highest moral values, not failing to embody them, as is true with this minister, who then left the church and now heads a Methodist denomination in another state" (47). She relates the pain of the transition but sees it now as a blessing, guiding her on her true path.

From what I have presented thus far, I cull from it as well as from Graham's text in order to pose the following questions for reflection:

- What is one example of what is most difficult for you to accept and/or to tolerate?
- Name one affliction you are suffering now or have in the past. What has been your response to it?
- How do you embrace or reject moral pain and suffering?
- What two examples represent the moral code you live by? What has changed in it over the years?
- Do you always know what is the right thing to do in all circumstances?
- When you are uncertain, how do you work with it?
- Are you capable of revising the moral terms of current cultural and global influences? Are you destined to be a victim of what is created for you to accept and abide by?
- Is there a conflict in your life that you have decided simply to live with, to tolerate and accept? Has the price tag been worth it?
- Does your life have a mission statement? I call them myth statements. Write it out. Mine, or one of mine: "In my serenity resides my sanity." Another: "Excess is access." Another: "Forgive yourself and others ten times a day if need be." Another: "Support others enthusiastically in their work or struggles."
- What do you trust today that you once distrusted?
- What do you distrust today that you once trusted?
- What kinds of current relations are you in with others on a regular basis?
- Where and when in your life are you violent or dismissive towards yourself? Towards others?
- Where and when in your life do you feel a desire or impulse to be violent towards others?

- If you were to consider making a change in your life based on something you have come to realize has been imposed on you, what would it be and what would it take to act on it?
- Is there a part of your life that you find frustrating or intolerable because of something you have left unlived?
- Recall an experience of dissociation when you disconnected, or felt coerced to abandon, a core part of yourself. Were you or are you able to reconnect with it or do you perhaps find it best not to? Or even need to?
- What fundamental truth in your life continues to assist your growth?
- Can you or do you wish to reconnect to something or someone that once excited and interested you?
- Are there people, situations, projects, or plans that at one time interested and excited you but no longer have that original Eros? What happened to them?
- Are there one or more habits of mind that you would like to change but have not yet succeeded in doing so? Habits of mind grow from parts of our personal myth that may have become calcified or that organically continue to serve us.
- Think of a life situation that encouraged or coerced you, or forced you to adapt, to change. What did you do or think in order to adapt?
- Can you recall an event, situation, person or persons where a core value you held was destabilized by contending alterations?
- Where, if you can identify it, does or has a moral injury located itself in the body? Moral injuries always implicate the body: we are always *soulbody* beings.
- Do you carry moral injuries stemming from ideas or beliefs in a god image who is hard to accept or creates conflicts? What is your god image?
- Describe a moral dilemma or dissonance you struggle with now. Is God part of this struggle?
- Can you imagine and devise an alternate frame to this moral struggle? What in it might need revisioning, which

may or may not insist on a moral reframing of your
beliefs?

- Do you find it impossible to talk to others who are
  committed to a different political position without
  enflaming one another?
- Where in your life generally are you least flexible?

Working with any of these questions will help to illuminate places in
your life where moral injuries are located and where healing
possibilities will open to you.

Works Cited

Campbell, Joseph. *Flight of the Wild Gander: Explorations in the
    Mythological Dimension. Selected Essays 1944-1968.* New World
    Library, 2002.

Graham, Larry Kent. *Moral Injury: Restoring Wounded Souls.* Abingdon
    Press, 2017.

Jung, C.G. *The Archetypes and the Collective Unconscious.* Vol. 9, i. *The
    Collected Works of C.G. Jung,* 2nd Edition. Edited by Herbert Read,
    Michael   Fordham, et. al., translated by R.F.C. Hull. Princeton
    UP, 1959/1971.

Lakoff, George. *Don't Think of an Elephant: Know Your Values and
    Frame Your Debate.* Chelsea Green Publishers, 2004.

Slattery, Dennis Patrick. *The Wounded Body: Remembering the Markings of
    Flesh.* SUNY P, 2000.

---. *Riting Myth, Mythic Writing: Plotting Your Personal Story.* Fisher King
    Press, 2012.

Tick, Edward. *Warrior's Return: Restoring the Soul After War.* Sounds
    True, 2014.

Whitmont, Edward C. *The Alchemy of Healing: Psyche and Soma.* North
    Atlantic Books, 1993.

Further Reading

Child, Barbara. *Memories of a Vietnam Veteran: What I Have Remembered
    and What He Could Not Forget.* Chiron Publications, 2019.

Chodron, Pema. *Taking the Leap: Freeing Ourselves from Old Habits and Fears*. Shambhala Publications, 2010.

---. *When Things Fall Apart: Heart Advice for Difficult Times*. Shambhala Publications, 2000.

Johnson, Robert. *Inner Work: Using Dreams and Active Imagination for Personal Growth*. HarperSanFrancisco, 1986.

Kendall, R.T. *Total Forgiveness*. Charisma House, 2002.

May, Gerald. *The Awakened Heart: Opening Yourself to the Love You Need*. HarperCollins, 1993.

McAdams, Dan P. *The Stories We Live By: Personal Myths and the Making of the Self*. Guilford Press, 1993.

Morrison. Toni. *The Origin of Others*. Harvard UP, 2017.

Steindl-Rast, Brother David. *Gratefulness, The Heart of Prayer: An Approach to Life in Its Fullness*. Paulist Press, 1984.

5

BORDERING ON BOLDNESS: THE WISDOM IN DEEP CREATIVITY[*]

*But don't be satisfied with stories, how things
have gone with others. Unfold
your own myth, without complicated explanation. . .*

~Rumi, "Unfold Your Own Myth," 41

I am so grateful to be here with you at this exciting and thoughtful conference. Two of the most creative people I know are in this room. As many of you have followed the offerings of both Aryeh Maidenbaum and Diana Rubin over the decades, you have watched their own myths unfold through their rich, varied and exciting creative work in the programs they have offered the world. So I cannot begin talking about creativity and its salvific effects on each of us without first acknowledging their work, and us as the beneficiaries of their continual largesse.

C.G. Jung writes that imagination is the door into the psychic realm. I would add to his powerful insight that myth is the corridor into that same terrain because myths carry their own way of imagining. We each embody a mythic imagination; it is most fundamentally a place

---

[*] Presented to the conference, "Jung on the Hudson," Rhinebeck, New York, July 17, 2018.

as well as a playful and purposeful response to life. It places us in a boundary of conjunctions between conscious and unconscious forces and presences. It may be inspired, roiled, irritated or activated by so many impingements both from within and without. It may arise from something we have experienced either literally or imaginally, in conversation with a friend or in experiencing a story through the powerful medium of film. Jung's famous process of individuation rests largely on the action of unfolding one's personal myth. Beginning this way, and having spent time these last seven months exploring Jung's *The Red Book*, I was tempted to make this presentation about his epic journey and struggle into the fathomless depths of his own psyche as well as into the world soul.

But I was led in another direction by influences I cannot name. In pursuit of my own creative trajectory at this stage in my life, I continue when possible to bring film into my talks. Three years ago, I presented Horton's Foote's *Tender Mercies* at this conference. Another film more recently came to my attention, suggested by a friend whose instincts I trust. The film is called *Paterson* and it outlines some dynamic aspects or dimensions of the creative process in the lives of a married couple, one a city bus driver in Paterson, New Jersey and the other his wife, who is engaged in another epic enterprise: Home-making. Both in their own ways are fully engaged in acts of *poiesis,* a beautiful Greek term that means a making or shaping something into a coherent form by re-presenting it. That making may mean giving a certain shape to a life, which may include creative acts of imagination that express themselves in painting, composing and performing music, shaping clay into various vessels and figures, cross-stitching, reading, writing or giving a meaningful shape to every day of one's life.

I encourage you to view this 2016 film, but especially through the template of individuation, the creative process and the mythologizing of an identity. Within this context, let me begin with a question: You recall that Jung's own language on individuation captures something of the title of this conference: "Looking back, Looking Forward: Reviewing and Reorienting Our Lives." Early on in his essay, "Conscious, Unconscious and Individuation" (1939/40, 275ff) Jung reminds us: "Individuation is a process by which a person becomes a psychological individual, a separate individual unity, or whole" (275).

Thank goodness he says nothing about becoming perfect, only whole. A big enough charge. But I am more interested in what he says five pages later, which may help us grasp the complexity of this conference: "The unconscious has a Janus face: one points back to the preconscious prehistoric world of instinct while the other anticipates the future" (279); and given that each of us contains unconsciously the whole development of our ancestors—it has an all-pervasive historic aspect. Now part of how I understand mythic consciousness is that it aids us in developing a substantial and meaningful relationship with the outer world of events with our inner world of psychic activity. One step further: the unconscious, as Jung describes it, also has both a historical and teleological impulse or energy thrust. Let's look a bit more closely at who and what Janus is. Much of the following is from an on-line source.

> Janus was one of the earliest of the Roman deities, sometimes referred to as the "god of gods" or *diuom deo;* others equated him with the Etruscan god Culcans. However, there are at least two notable myths concerning his origin. And, according to both, unlike other Roman and Greek gods, Janus may have actually lived. In the first myth, he ruled alongside an early Roman king named Camesus. After Janus' exile from Thessaly (a province in northern Greece), he arrived in Rome with his wife Camise or Camasnea and children, the most notable being Tiberinus (god of the Tiber). Shortly after arriving, he built a city on the west bank of the Tiber called the Janiculum. According to some, he was the custodian of the universe but, to all Romans, he was the god of beginnings and endings, presiding over every entrance and departure. Because every door and passageway looks in two directions, Janus was seen as two-faced or *Janus bifrons*— the god who looked both ways.

> He was the gatekeeper; his symbols were a porter's staff or *virga* and a set of keys. To illustrate his importance, his name was even mentioned before Jupiter in prayers. He protected the start of all activities. He inaugurated the seasons. The first day of each month was considered sacred to him but the first month of the year—January—which many consider named in his honor—was actually named

for Juno, queen of the gods. Early Romans coins featured his image, showing him as two-faced, one bearded and one clean-shaven. Later, during the Renaissance, this image of two faces would represent not only the past and future but also wisdom. https://www.ancient.eu/Janus/

It would seem a good idea when we reflect on our past and reshape our future by means of it, that we keep Janus close by; he is that inaugurating force that is, I sense, a key player in the desires of our own creativity, our impulse to leave a trace, to make a mark and to be re-membered in both an individual and social context. He calls to us in our recollections and in our anticipations as well as bridges the two creative acts of remembrance and renewal.

I will end this slight excursion into myth and into this crucial mythic figure by calling back to our consciousness a line from *Dream Analysis: Notes of the Seminar Given in 1928-30.* There Jung and two, maybe three colleagues, are wrestling with a middle-aged man's short dream, contained in some 6-7 sentences. In the midst of associating with its images, Jung begins to riff on the spiralic quality of nature, possibly influenced by some of Goethe's *Botanical Writings.* Jung then offers the following profound insight: "Psychologically you develop in a spiral, you always come over the same point where you have been before, but it is never exactly the same, it is either above or below" (*Dream* 100). And then you move on. I think Janus may be here as well, even though the spiral does not have doorways; however, it does have a dual motion back and forth, a movement forward and a swinging back, but never to where we were. And then a repeated forward motion.

Within the geometry of the spiral, I am fascinated and have to wonder about this connection between creativity and wisdom. This latter term is hard to define, even harder to find, or discover. From my perch, wisdom seems to be encouraged by openness, a certain attitude to things of the world, one that emanates from acceptance of the way things are. Jung observes that "attitude is a readiness of the psyche to act or react in a certain way. . . . To have an attitude means to be ready for something definite, even though this something is unconscious" (*CW* 6, p. 414). Of course, they can be changed, altered, and even improved, but first, to accept the way things are seems wise. Wisdom seems also connected to one's ability to notice the small, the particular, the incidental, even the nuances inherent in the world's matter, which includes our own mattering.

Wisdom has much to do with our own creative processes, which are intimately tied to our on-going progression of awakening, of individuating, and of our desire to be part of a larger community. Each of our creative processes, with their own vitality, springs from a creative tension within: a gap, a fissure, a space, yearning to be fulfilled, not simply filled. That gap exists between what is invisible within me and what is outside me; a breach is a gap in the sense that it can mean a form of birthing and a form of breaking from the waters of the unconscious much as a humpback whale, for instance, will breach in the Pacific waters off the coast of Santa Barbara, California. At that moment of breaching, the whale unites two worlds, the watery cosmos of its habitation as well as the air we breathe; in breaching it sees what it cannot when swimming. It must shift its angle of perception from horizontal to vertical to open it to a greater worldview.

It may be that our creative breaches call to us with more assertiveness in our more mature years. It is in part the call to where our lives remain unlived and perhaps yet unresolved. I use the image of the breaching whale to suggest something of the underworld of the unconscious. When the whale breaches, it enjoys an instant when it can look backward and forward in a panoramic survey of what still yearns to be lived. I want to call this moment an insight of longing, of yearning, to be completed but not perfected. D. Stephenson Bond writes in *Living Myth* that it is the potential for development of what Jung called the restless urge of the psyche to realize itself more fully and completely, which is the deciding factor (66). It is, he goes on, a "core" experience of life, a decisive moment, which is the raw material of myth.

In a book that I co-authored with two eminently creative people, Deborah Ann Quibell and Jennifer Leigh Selig, *Deep Creativity: Seven Ways to Spark Your Creative Spirit,* we identified more than a dozen traits or attributes of what Deep Creativity engenders and promotes. I offer a small handful here for you to consider: Deep Creativity

- Is archetypal
- Is alchemical
- Is receptive
- Is emotional

- Is healing
- Is autonomous
- Is participatory
- Is embodied
- Is ensouled (*Deep Creativity* 321-25)

Something seeks expression and we are chosen, then called upon to do so. It is a vocation in the sense of being called to both a context (a particular field) and a content (the matter at hand). My sense here is that wisdom and creativity find a common territory when barriers weaken or collapse and an authentic openness floods our attention. This creative urge includes a deepening and furthering of individuation—which I understand as becoming more aware of wisdom's constant presence in us, our deepest reservoir of wisdom. Such a creative urge encourages mindfulness and a healing of the rifts in our life, but not the gaps. We need the gaps to breathe in, then out, as Deborah Anne Quibell describes it in our book mentioned above. Creativity encourages a deeper form of awakening, which I will illustrate with a story from my own life that was an "AHA" moment in capital letters. I sense that what we are awakened to, in large measure, is the present moment, the most authentic place of our existence. The following poem had at its intention to give this urge a voice:

Dream the Prize

See what you have
Dive before the watercourse
Shrinks into shallows.
Find the thread that unravels
Back to the shirt you are wearing
Travel south of anger
West of resentment
North of desire and
East of envy—
. . . .

At night, find a bridge to sleep
Beneath

Watch for the prize
It will float in the dark silent
Silk river just feet from
Where you dream (*Road, Frame, Window* 95).

Just a few more reflections on this deeply complex relationship between creativity and wisdom. All creative acts have their own manner of recreating the world. Some crucial and essential levels or dimensions of the world are altered by our creative projects and achievements. Some divine presence enters our creative space, our field of *influence* and *confluence,* and there the wisdom lies dormant, ready to be invited in; its origin is another realm that in-spirits us in creating. In this creative act we recreate ourselves and move closer to our full image of Self. Jennifer Leigh Selig treats this rich imaginative act of recreation in her insightful chapter, "To Create is to Re-Create: Repairing and Restorying Childhood Suffering" (160-73). Individuation is an on-going act of creation, a truth Jung's *The Red Book* offers on every page. One of the most moving illustrations, from my reading, is Jung's connection with the dead who come to him, just as they gathered around Odysseus and his men in Hades in Homer's *Odyssey.*

The dead in Jung's world are far from happy; they wish to live some part of their lives they missed or ignored or were so tangled in the lives of others that they defected from their true calling. In their hunger and despair, they teach us of something ontological in our creative life, which is so intimate with a completed life. Jung's encounter with those who seek his advice and consolation carry implicitly this question: right now, what have I not done that I always yearned to do, accomplish, see, experience? Individuation is a form of renewal or re-creation of ourselves in an uncertain life with no real guarantees.

I ask you to test these observations with the following question: what motivates you or spurs you on to create, even if that creation is your life you sculpt each day? And then, how does this on-going project nourish you? Is there something uncompleted that you sense you must finish in order to fulfill something in yourself? Have you heard or been prompted by the call to create but refused the call, chose not to heed it, instead responding: "Call me back, I'm busy now?" In your studies, did you heed the call of a discipline or subject you loved? Did you choose a safer, more acceptable path, something more practical? Where are you now with that decision? Or, what were you stirred to learn that you passed by? And conversely, what were you stirred to learn that you heeded?

I end with words of one of the coauthors of *Deep Creativity*, Deborah, who gives eloquent voice to the power of depth and creativity that we kept our focus on in creating *Deep Creativity*. "We use this term to capture, invoke, and (re)inspire a style of creativity that is not horizontal, skating the surface of experience like the water strider, but instead is vertical, moving down into the depths of one's soul and coming up with a spirited creative expression" ("Introduction" 4). Such a form of creativity is itself individuating the soul into its own elegant awareness. Jung understood this deep aesthetic urge to "make something of yourself" in the world. These reflections have attempted to give a further voice to such a noble human pilgrimage that is never fully completed.

Works Cited

Bond, D. Stephenson. *Living Myth: Personal Meaning as a Way of Life*. Shambhala Publications, 2007.

Donohue, Timothy, Donald Carlson and Dennis Patrick Slattery. *Road, Frame, Window: A Poetics of Seeing*. Mandorla Books, 2015.

Jung, C.G. *Dream Analysis: Notes of the Seminar Given in 1928-30*. Edited by William McGuire. Bollingen Series XCIX. Princeton UP, 1984.

---. *The Archetypes and the Collective Unconscious*. Vol. 9i. *The Collected Works of C. G. Jung*. Translated by R.F.C. Hull. 2nd Edition. 1971.

---. *Psychological Types*. Vol. 6. *The Collected Works of C.G. Jung*. Sir Herbert Read, Michael Fordham, et.al, editors, a revision by R.F.C. Hull of the translation by H.G. Baynes. 1990.

Quibell, Deborah Anne, Jennifer Leigh Selig and Dennis Patrick Slattery. *Deep Creativity: Seven Ways to Spark Your Creative Spirit*. Shambhala Publications, 2019.

The Essential Rumi. Translated by Coleman Barks, with John Moyne, et. al., Castle Books, 1997.

Further Reading

Apostolos-Cappadona, Diane, editor. *Art, Creativity, and the Sacred.* Continuum, 1996.

Cameron, Julia. *The Complete Artist's Way: Creativity as a Spiritual Practice.* Jeremy Tarcher/Penguin, 2007.

Loori, John Daido. *The Zen of Creativity: Cultivating Your Artistic Life.* Ballantine Books, 2004.

Steiner, Rudolf. *Art as Spiritual Activity. Selected Lectures on the Visual Arts.* Anthroposophic Press, 1998.

6

THE BULL ON THE PAGE AND THE BULL ON THE PAVEMENT: REFLECTIONS ON JAMES HILLMAN'S *ANIMAL PRESENCES*[*]

Consider animals: how just they are, how well-behaved, how they keep to the time-honored, how loyal they are to the land that bears them, . . . how they care for their young, how they go together to pasture, and how they draw one another to the spring.

~C.G. Jung (2009). *The Red Book: A Readers Edition*, 341

One of the joys and challenges of reading any of James Hillman's works is to notice *(notitia)* what he provokes, invokes and evokes in us as readers. Reading him has always felt to me like dreaming in a landscape that has some familiarity but is also slants precipitously into strangeness. *Animal Presences* pushed me to understand more deeply the animal in dream as well as the animals that surround me. The volume could easily be entitled *Animal Presents,* for the deepened insights he offers feel like gifts to be understood through our own life experiences via dreams, daily life and works of art, fiction and music.

Now it feels risky to me to begin this presentation by relating a bunch of bull, most precisely in an encounter with a loose bull in our rural neighborhood about a year ago. As I began to read chapter two,

---

[*] Presented at the conference on James Hillman's *Animal Presences,* The Dallas Institute of Humanities and Culture, Dallas, Texas. October 26-27, 2018.

"Imagination is Bull," I realized that there might be a place for my own bull to play a role in understanding two elements in the book: amplification as a form of deepening and broadening one's understanding, as well as the many faces that an image can assume through such a process; not so much a process, really, as an imaginal engagement with a literal occurrence that unfastened further ways of understanding what I can only call at the beginning here as a numinous experience.

But in saying this I have already broken a cardinal tenet of Hillman's method. For what he says of dream images can be applied to experiences that have the pulse of a waking dream, which is what I believe I experienced. He tells us that "a dream brings with it a terrible urge for understanding" (18). But we might want to withhold that urge initially for if "we can hold back the hermeneutic desire so that the image can elaborate itself" (18), we may move closer to its reality, not ours. He follows this observation with the key question that permeates, and I believe guides, the entire volume: "If so, then does amplification help the image and how?" (18). But first to my bull:

My wife and I live outside the city of New Braunfels, Texas midway between San Antonio and Austin in what is still called "the Hill Country." Each lot is five acres or more. Ranchers' spreads mingle with residential homes, most of which are fenced and gated, which will become important in a moment. There is very little traffic even in the early morning hours when people who have not retired are headed to work. My wife and I have discovered five different walks through this rural landscape that we can choose from and enjoy any given morning.

On one particular early morning I headed out from our home alone, having chosen a route that roundtrip takes about an hour. It was a peaceful Monday morning, with clear skies, no wind and a multitude of birds entertaining one another in the trees on both sides of the street with no sidewalks, as is the rule in this rural terrain. I made it to the turn-around along Isaac Creek Road and began the mile and a half hike back to our home. I approached the only piece of property that had not yet been built on or fenced in, as were all the other lots on the street. It was still thick with live oaks and mountain laurels.

The silence and serenity of the air was abruptly disturbed by a thundering crash from deep within the lot. Then, in an instant, a large, excited and thrashing bull charged out in front of me by only a few yards, passed me by and came to a halt in the middle of the road just a short distance from where I was walking. He may have been as frightened as I was, so animated was he; he swung his large head back and forth, making the white plastic tags identifying who he belonged to slap against his ears and nose to which they were stapled. The morning sun shone on his magnificent tan hide as he came into the sunlight out of the shadowed lot. He had, as I said, stopped abruptly in the middle of the street, turned toward me and slowed his movements. He then became very quiet and gazed at where I had gone.

When he charged out of the lot, my legs took over and turned me into where he had emerged; it was the only place where I could immediately put some distance and obstacles in the form of large trees between us. I remember being both calm and terrified when I realized that he was not planning to run any farther but had halted and collected himself and now watched me for what *my* next move would be. When I had turned into the lot and put a large live oak between us, I looked back at his face, now calm and still and studying me less with fear than with curiosity. At this point I find it difficult to describe what I saw in that face and superbly powerful body. But as I recall the incident, I remember thinking at the moment what I sensed as a felt thought or an embodied knowing or a visceral discovery: in front of me is a god, a divinity. No, it was less a thought than a felt revelation, a visitation of a reality that was the bull. I did not lose the bull in the idea of a god, nor did the god separate from the bull's magnificence, his power, his fully engaged presence. They were one. I felt like a subject in the presence of a force or presence that was numinous.

I remember thinking too of his animal scent as he disturbed the air just yards in front of me when he bolted from the wooded lot. I heard the deepness of his breathing as his startled bulk whooshed by me, then halted and raised that glorious head, snapping back and forth and the slapping of the plastic property tags he wore as they smacked against his skin. I heard as well the powerful thuds of his hooves as he ran in front of me, the moist soil that his hooves kicked up, as well as the cracking of a few branches in the trees around him when he rushed from the shadows of the vacant lot.

But what remained most mysterious and awesome was his huge elegant head that snorted in surprise and his eyes wide with astonishment at my presence on the street before I had ducked instinctively into the woods seeking cover. Neither of us had expected one another: he who had escaped from a broken gate the rancher had neglected about a half mile from where we both stood now, and I on a morning stroll. I want to say in retrospect that at the moment I did not conceptualize the bull into a deity; that reality was present in the flesh of the bull, in his power, his magnitude and in his sheer presence. Lots of bull gathered on the road as an overwhelming presence.

I have asked myself since that experience while reading *Animal Presences,* especially Chapter Two, what was revealed to me in that instant, for that is how long it took to unfurl—an instant. For that moment awakened something in me; it included senses of confusion, threat and creativity—all in a heap. It made me glad to be alive, especially in the presence of an animal that I believed would do me harm if I did not move with some dispatch. I also sensed that this incident was a gifted moment. I felt something of my own animal body commune with the bull's presence, with its thick energy, its presence as an emanation, an emanation that inspired. I felt in my bones something of the bull's majesty, its fierce combustion, its fiery frenzy, followed by its regal calm and curiosity.

Hiding now behind some trees in the vacant lot, I looked across to the street where he stood, like a king gazing at one of his frightened subjects. I did not ask myself, in recollecting on this moment of encounter, what the bull "meant" or what the entire experience's significance was. I was still transfixed in my body with that instant when I recognized in the bull's shaking head, his asserting of himself, another dimension of being—of spirit, of grandeur, of a majestic presence. Words fail to carry the impact of that moment, but I believed, given Hillman's extraordinary imagination as well as his method of perceiving by analogies with a host of disciplines that serve him as corridors into amplifying what he explores, that some connection to my experience might be of real value. He then cites Jung's understanding of the alchemists who used amplification and analogy to bring an experience that was vague or obscure "to the point of intelligibility" (qtd. in Hillman 19).

With this story as my baseline, or my line of bull, I read and engaged Chapter Two in search of what could be a furthering of this moment with its implications, correspondences and associations. Perhaps in some ways amplification is a form of animalization. Amplifying as animalizing. Amplification as a particularly unique form of an imagination. "Abase yourself and live your animal so that you will be able to treat your brother correctly," Jung encourages us in *The*

Red Book (342).[1] His words encourage us to connect with it and be it, for we carry an animal imagination in us that most emphatically makes us more, not less, human.

Few other volumes of Hillman's writing carry the playfulness with language and with cultural metaphors as does *Animal Presences*. Right out of the chapter's chute he hones in on The Dallas Institute's own reasons for being—a splendid locale for bull—in fact a home to express "the curious confusion of imagination and bull" (58). "Hercules, too, is a bully and a bull-slinger" (60). "Bull is good for your health" (61); with the onrush of a bull "we are cowed in its presence" (61); "Myth, after all, is what is said about what is said: the bull about the bull" (63); "Even when their [economists] pronouncements are dressed in statistics we sense they are full of bull" (65); "the same old bull is continuing as we make up myths that account for our foundations . . ." (66). And more seriously, "from the heroic Mithra to the subtle passivity and imaginative fertility of the Christ figure who assumes the place of the sacrificial animal gives a founding mythic power, the fertility of bull, to the Christian imagination" (73).

The bull in myth, history, culture, literature and religion serves most prominently and primitively as a founding animal, an animal at the gates of origins, of beginnings, including the alphabet. Few animals have such deep and consistent relations with the imagination itself, as Hillman observes towards the end of his chapter. Cultural impulses may continue to slash and slay the bull, "make mincemeat of it," which has its analogy in "cutting out imagination as a confusing variable. But bull keeps coming—inflating its killers" (74). Our work as well as the work of the Institute is to "become disciples of bull, creating and shaping imagination, riding its back by hanging on, propitiating with our words, our very talk, our 'b.s.' . . ." (75). That "s" of the "b.s." I would argue, might place us within the field of a new form of relating to the bull: let's call it a Residual Psychology, an excremental way of seeing, whose angle of vision towards waste is accompanied by a sense of wonder.

While one could argue that the largest animal in the pages of *Animal Presences* is the imagination itself in its subtle workings, its positive power to find analogies for both being and becoming, underneath is the value of the image itself both self-contained and in motion, as Faulkner said of our human capacity and propensity. Amplification may also be a form of "archetypal activism," a term that guides much of Mary Watkins' writing and work in the classroom, working with inmates and encouraging students to active participation in the world's suffering.

In an essay that might serve as a useful accompaniment to *Animal Presences* is James' brilliant essay, "An Inquiry into Image," which can be read as a foundational and originary document of what archetypal psychology is and is not. I returned to it not only to think further on my own bull story but on the entirety of *Animal Presences*. Everything hinges on the nature and function of the image as it is lived and researched, since research is one of the cornerstones of a depth psychological knowing. As such, it has many cross-references to poetic, or better, mythopoetic knowledge that Gaston Bachelard, who James names as one of the founding voices of archetypal psychology, so carefully enumerates in his writings.

For Hillman, "'archetypal' does value the image by pointing to fecundity (Langer) and generativity (Erikson). We need the terms to encourage our searching, to make us feel the transcending importance of the image" (83). As an adjective, he points out, this psychology is one of value, of valuing. An important element in Bachelard's own thought surfaces here: valorization. His translator, Colette Gaudin, writes in a footnote to a section of *The Psychoanalysis of Fire* that the term "is defined as '*the act of acquiring or attributing a value.*' Valorization and valoriser are key words for the methodology developed in Bachelard's works. They refer to the spontaneous activity of imagination attributing subjective values to its objects" (*On Poetic Imagination and Reverie* (4-5, note 2). Here I am thinking of my experience recited earlier. I did not want to move the image of the bull into the terrain of symbol or concept, but to stay with its presence as well as I understand that term. My hope here was not to transform *the* bull into *my* bull and lose in the process its fullness of presence. My subjective experience need not become *that* personal!

Bachelard's valorizing has its analogy in one use of the word "archetypal" for which Hillman offers a series of descriptors: "unfathomable, patterned, hidden, rich, prior, deep, necessary, permanent. These are the words we have used to give a sense of value" (1977, p. 83). Archetypal psychology is a form of adjectival knowing, a psychology of qualities and I would add, qualitative presences. It is concerned with the subjectivity of experience reinforced by research that enlarges the orbit of that experience. And further in the same discussion, he writes: "'Archetypal' here refers to a move one makes rather than a thing that is. Otherwise, archetypal psychology becomes only a psychology of archetypes" (83). When the noun overshadows the adjective, another form of understanding slips into the imagination that loses the qualitative move and ushers in another form of amplification, one that may simplify the phenomenon even as it magnifies its dimensions. In the word "archetypal" there is a halo of alternatives as well as correspondences surrounding its use. A penumbric psychology? They may include, as Hillman writes, "mythical, religious, institutional, instinctual, philosophical, or literary" dimensions (83). Archetypal psychology is then an alternative psychology, one which is fluid, protean, elastic, adaptive, multi-valanced, even mysterious in its forms of mythopoetic expression.

Its on-going mythology hosts a series of corridors down which one might pilgrimage to see in a glass of multiple mirrors pieces of relevance, shards of value, segments of significance, all of which add to the fullness of the image, which is where all exploration begins and ends. So the title of the book, *Animal Presences,* is such an apt one in keeping with the adjectival nature of archetypal psychology and its modes of amplification of an experience's qualities. To amplify is less to *clarify* than it is to *multiply* values that correspond and that are there in the image, often hidden from plain sight. *The Presence of Animals* as an alternate title would have violated one of the founding notions of archetypal psychology: the multiple expressions of value and quality as modifiers of a psychology that wishes to avoid: "pointing at something rather than pointing to something" (82), most especially its worth, unrelated to the driving forces of commodities and commerce.

About a third of the way through his bull essay, Hillman reminds us: "I have been proposing an equation: bull=imagination. But not all imagination is bull. I would locate our bull in a specific place, the non-place of origins. . . "(*Animal* 64). The bull sits or sidles through the origins and ground of culture "and its inseminating starting point" (64). Myth is then indeed bull; perhaps its evacuations mythically sensed is history. Bull and its shit, then, is the *prima materia* of civilization culturally-construed. The bull's prowess and its evacuations bespeak two forms of fecundity, one of the sustaining values of archetypal psychology.

My bull moment as I walked in our neighborhood and encountered such a magnificent animal who had successfully broken loose from its captivity, its fenced-in life, may have been a moment of joy and surprise, even shock for both of us. He in his newly-earned freedom, I in my fright seeking a place to contain and protect me; in short, a home like the one he escaped from. A certain amount of energy that I would describe as awe may have passed between us. I think as well that what I discerned in his majestic face and powerful eyes was the beginning of something, some originary experience that this animal alone carried in his physiological and cultural history. For an instant, he slowed just enough to allow me to participate in the non-place of myth that he carried in every muscle of his unsettling image.

Endnotes

[1]The reader may find Jung's further observations on learning to assimilate one's animal as well as the value of animals' behavior in footnote 180 on p. 342.

Works Cited

Bachelard, Gaston. *On Poetic Imagination and Reverie*. Translated by Collette Gaudin. Spring Publications, 1987.
---. *The Psychoanalysis of Fire*. Translated by Alan C.M. Ross. Beacon Press, 1964.
Hillman, James. *Animal Presences*. Spring Publications, 2008.
---. "An Inquiry into Image." *Spring: An Annual of Archetypal Psychology and Jungian Thought*. Spring Publications, 1977, pp. 62-87.
Jung, C.G. *The Red Book, Liber Novus. A Reader's Edition*. Translated by Mark Kyburz, John Peck, et. al., edited by Sonu Shamdasani. Philemon Series. W.W. Norton, 2009.

ץ

PHOTOGRAPHY AND
PAINTING[*]

I cannot thank Stephanie Pope enough for making space for a series
of blogs that she has introduced. It affords me the opportunity to play
with the difference and similarities between a photo of a scene in
nature and a subsequent creation of that scene in an acrylic painting
that I am currently completing. They are, in Aristotle's term, two
different forms of *techne*. Here is the background to frame the blog's
content.

I recently traveled to Cleveland, Ohio to visit family and friends.
My younger brother Bill and I have some favorite walking and hiking
trails east of Cleveland in Chardon, Ohio that we try to frequent daily.
One in particular, part of the Metropolitan Park system, is Strawberry
Lane, which includes both horse trails as well as firmer asphalt
walkways that stretch for many miles into beautiful wooded terrains,
the Chardon river, and peaceful lagoons. Depending on our energy
level and the climate, we choose one or the other. On this particular
morning, we chose to walk several miles along an asphalt path that
meanders through the woods, alongside lakes and rivers, a few swamp
sites, then on into a series of rolling hills.

We are never in a hurry, so we pause often on our hike. On one
of these walks, I am arrested by the way the morning sun slants
through the trees along our path; we stop to let the image work on and
over us. It is a very quiet morning with few fellow hikers and little
traffic on this weekday, so we enjoy the silence and solitude as well.
After a few minutes, I pull out my smartphone and *capture the scene* in

---

* Blog on Stephanie Pope's www. mythopoetics.com.

an instant. I take several shots of it, even as it continues to change slightly with the sun's movement and the trees' shadows. Later I will ask myself: what am I after in *taking* these photos? What am I *giving* in return? It is pleasurable now to *have* the scene in my phone to enjoy whenever I like. I may, for instance, when I return home, print it out and place it behind a frame to hang in my study. Or I may, after a time, simply delete it to make room for other photos.

Strawberry Lane, Chardon, Ohio.

My question at this point is: is the above a representation of nature? Is it the scene frozen in an instant? Did taking the photo involve a creative act or process? Have the woman and her dog receding from the photo stopped aging, now frozen in time? It is true that something about this scene arrested me: the lighting, the dark shadows of the trunks reaching skyward, the woman walking her small dog, the many nuanced shades of green and the dappled or mottled asphalt path. Did I bring something into being through the framed image I clicked into permanence on my phone? A moment later the light is different and the scene I captured on my phone is gone, for good, as we say. I do not know if I created anything here, or just simply recorded in one instant in time a scene offered to me, and I *took* it. I took advantage of its presence. Now I *have* it. What does that mean?

So I have to wonder if this image qualifies as a mimetic image of nature, namely, some creation or even recreation of nature growing out of, as Aristotle believes, a natural human instinct. Or is it more simply and mundanely a mechanical or technological reproduction and I should not claim anything creative about its genesis as a photo? I was perhaps only at the right place at the right time. On the other hand, of all the myriad scenes we passed through that morning, I chose this one *to take* so to remember it and the beautiful day with my brother, so something creative is at work here; but what?

Mimesis, as Aristotle defines it, characterizes the axis between the artist and his/her creation growing out of a natural human instinct to make something. Is the act of *taking the photo* an artistic one? It may be truer to surmise that the photo is more a correspondence or an accord between an aspect of reality, now reconstructed in a medium as close as possible in equivalence to the viewed/experienced scene. Nature designed the scene and I recorded a segment of the total landscape. Is that about it?

At one point Aristotle suggests that some mimetic works have a cognitive significance that goes beyond particulars to embody universals, which I believe we can also refer to as archetypes defined by C.G. Jung as a corelative. But I also wonder of the photo: is there a *poiesis*, or a making of something present in it? Did I make something of *nature* through taking it by means of *culture*'s technology? Depending on how one responds to these questions, a third may intrude itself: Is the photo a duplication of nature or a correspondence of it? Sorry about all the questions: I seem to have more of them than assertions.

The world seems more interesting from such an interrogative perspective. Taking the photo has made me curious about what I have actually achieved.

So let's see what happens when we turn to the painting that grew from this photo; it is in its final stages at this moment.

I want to show it in this form, in process, yet nearing completion. I want to note at the outset that I had no desire to create an accurate copy of the photo, but to revision the subject matter in a burst of painterly license. The acrylic painting has been in process for months. It required painting a backdrop of the sky; then, beginning at the back of the canvas (16x20), layering in the trees in three dimensions to give the *illusion* of depth. Now this procedure is closer, I believe, to an aesthetic act of making, what Aristotle would call both a *poiesis* and a *mimesis*. It is a mimetic act. I wonder as well if it is not a mythic act of making as well, for my own personal myth is active in this process—choosing what to include, how to change parts of the original, what to finish at each sitting, and the like. Not incidentally, it also includes a *techne,* which my able and generous art instructor, Linda Calvert Jacobson, coaches me in. More truly, I see it as an analogy of the photo which is a copy, or replica of a scene in nature, in an instant of nature's presence as I framed it within the lens of my smart phone. Layers and layers of reality coalescing.

Aristotle suggests more than once that central to mimesis is "an imitation of Nature" on some level. The painting, he would affirm, is not an expression of *me*, the artist. Something more is at stake here in the mimetic interplay of photo and painting. I am not painting my interior but something more—an idea of reality not foreign to the trees and grass of nature in conjunction with the participation of culture, but more an analogy of them with its own order and arrangement; present is both inflection and particularity.

Yes, I continue to refer to the photo constantly as I create the painting, but I am after its characteristics, the light falling on the path in a particular way, for instance, or the pattern the trees assume in their richness and in relation to one another. The painting corresponds to and assimilates what the camera captured of nature in the photo. But it has its own form independent of the photo. Can I say the same of the photo? Does it too have an underlying form given that it is a product of technology *and* my own aesthetic delight? Both the photo and the painting do not depend on me to exist; they both exist independent of me. I mediated them into being. In that respect they are both mythic if one understands myth as a formed expression of mediating two realities—both inner and outer terrains that comprise me and which I participate in without pause. Both continue to give me, and I hope others, a certain aesthetic pleasure not divorced from the painting's achievement.

When I saw the scene in nature, I wanted to capture it directly, not to own it, necessarily, but to have it as a reproduction of my experience on the hiking trail with my brother. When I chose the photo as my subject matter for the painting, I knew I wanted to create an analogy of it with a series of mixes of acrylic paint and not a little help from my patient artist teacher. We all have an instinct, Aristotle observes, from childhood on to engage in mimesis. Rooted in human nature, mimesis is implicit in distinctively human patterns of action, so both the photo and painting carry a mythic element. I believe as well, in ways I cannot articulate, that they carry some presence of grace. They certainly carry my deep gratitude for their presence.

In addition, they both arose out of some desire, some impulse to recreate both mimetic acts: photographing the scene or painting it. I find a certain, but different, aesthetic pleasure in viewing both creations; each may reflect or mirror or correspond to some universal quality that we sense is present. Painting, music, pottery, writing, all yield mimetic art, as Aristotle observes. I wonder how Aristotle would judge photographs? I think that first of all he would find a photograph astonishing and wonder-ful.

He certainly found both understanding and wonder to comprise deep instinctive properties of being human: understanding because it fulfills our nature; wonder because it fulfills a desire to learn. I find that there is something to learn and to wonder about when comparing these two art forms, two corridors to making something new. Something has been re-freshed, including my sense of being alive and creative and ways that push me to risk something and even allow for failure in the process, always inherently present that offers no resolute certificate of guarantee. But if risk is not part of the process, then why bother?

Works Cited

Aristotle. *Poetics*. Translated by S.H. Butcher. Introduction by Francis Ferguson. Hill and Wang, 1969.

Further Reading

Gombrich, E.H. *Art and Illusion: A Study in the Psychology of Pictorial Representation,* 9th edition. Princeton UP, 2000.

Isaacson, Walter. *Leonardo Da Vinci.* Simon and Schuster, 2017.

The Art of C.G. Jung. Edited by the Foundation of the Works of C.G. Jung. Translated by Paul David Young and Christopher John Murray. Norton, 2019.

Maritain, Jacques. *Creative Intuition in Art and Poetry.* The A.W. Mellon Lectures in the Fine Arts, National Gallery of Art, Washington. Bollingen Series XXXV.1. Pantheon Books, 1955.

8

FROM WAR TO WONDER AND THE EPIC TRADITION[*]

I am happy to be back at The University of the Incarnate Word in San Antonio and to be speaking to you this afternoon about my new book, *From War to Wonder: Recovering Your Personal Myth Through Homer's* Odyssey.

What amazes me about literary classics such as Homer's epic is that after 3000 years it still speaks to us both personally and culturally. In addition, it is constantly retranslated by historical ages and finds new expressions over the centuries. Emily Wilson's recent translation of the *Odyssey* marks the first translation by a woman that we know of. There are also discussions about the authorship of this epic being a woman as well. But that is not my topic for today.

Rather, I want to speak about three areas that interest me: 1) the nature of epic; 2) the nature of myth, both personal and collective; 3) the act of reading as itself a mythological activity of imagination. I also believe that reading can be a spiritual practice, but that would require another presentation, which I would welcome. I have been interested for years, ever since graduate school at the University of Dallas in their Institute of Philosophic Studies in the early 1970s, in what kind of knowledge literature offers us? This question was first posed to us by Dr. Louise Cowan, who remained for many of us an influential mentor for decades afterwards. I had never heard such a question in all my years of taking courses in literature. She went on to ask us: What is its

[*] Lecture presented at The University of the Incarnate Word, San Antonio, Texas February 11th, 2020

mode of knowing that makes it distinct from other disciplines? To her penetrating musings, I would add my own: how does poetic knowledge contribute to shaping our personal myth that defines our deepest identity?

Literary classics, she continued, are a knowing by analogy, by metaphor, symbol, likeness, comparison. Said another way, these classic stories offer us knowledge, depending on our level of engagement with them. And its most perduring terrain, as the American novelist William Faulkner informs us, is the human heart in conflict or in confluence with itself and its surroundings; it is always seeking to find the right fit within a larger community and to construct a life story that most reflects this connection, this confluence and, yes, its spikes of conflict.

Generally, and world-wide, some deep attraction to narratives has been its landscape. Literature tells us stories. The most basic form of human expression is to tell or listen to stories so to further create one's identity in the world. Narratives define us and they shape/are shaped by our personal myth, often in conflict and at times in cahoots with the cultural myth we are imbedded in and cannot escape. But choosing which parts of it to accept, what to put on the shelf or leave on the side of life's highway, is our option, and indeed, our obligation.

We have learned that the word *myth* in Greek means plot. It is a structure, a narrative scaffolding, around which we build our life story. So, the plot of our lives is comprised of the myths we tell ourselves and others about ourselves, whether the stories be true or false. But we must always follow up by asking: true or false for whom? The stories we tell and read and hear on some level, if we are reflective, imitate or mimic our own lives, by the power of analogy, correspondence and accord. Said another way, they re-present our lives in an aesthetic form, and there is an intrinsic pleasure in that. Narratives are forms of knowing in its most basic and perhaps most entertaining vessel. We each have a deep and profound narrative nature, but it is often not cultivated to the extent that it could be to reveal ourselves to ourselves, and then to others. Here are a few short-hand observations about this topic that we can ponder if there is time.

- We can learn more deeply about ourselves through stories, especially the classics of literature, but we are not limited to them.

- It is amazing to me that a story crafted 3000 years ago can be more relevant to our current lives than a story we heard or read that was created a month ago.
- Stories can touch our imaginations in profound ways and open us to parts of ourselves we did not know existed or, more seriously, parts that we have for years, even decades, deflected or misinterpreted.
- Stories disclose us to ourselves and others in all our wonder and all our woundedness. We want to be always alert and prudent about the kinds of stories we tell ourselves. They can be extremely destructive, even self-sabotaging; they can also be nourishing and life-affirming.
- One of the benefits of reading and contemplating classic stories of literature is that they can advance us in self-knowledge, a project we can and should spend our lives exploring, editing, reframing and re-affirming.
- Reading literature can begin to open us to the myth we are living and in turn is living us. We can, with a meditative mind, sense its likeness to our own basic narrative, and perhaps exercise some revisioning of it to suit where and who we are now instead of continuing to live an image of ourselves whose shelf-life expired months or years ago.

Let me say just a few words about myth as I understand it. I will use the same shorthand here:

- A myth is that element or quality that holds our life in a complex network of coherences, conflicts and contradictions.
- Not to know the contours of our own myth can leave deep gaps in our identity and continued confusion where there may exist an underlying clarity.
- It gives our life purpose and meaning; a myth-less life is a life without meaning, and in some cases, without value because not recognized or appreciated.
- To begin to grasp our personal myth, we can reflectively ask: Who am I? Where am I going? What is my real passion in life? These are mythological questions, and perhaps spiritual ones as well.

- The beliefs that we hold dear help to concentrate our mythic selves into a unity while not denying where diversity, otherness and patterns of continued growth are operating.
- A myth is what we continually call on to create a functional relationship with the external world we move through daily as well as the interior terrain that comprises who/what we are and are becoming.
- A myth reveals to us our reference points in life. These reference points can be understood as our reverence points as well. What we reverence we reference, especially in times of hardship, loss or confusion.
- A myth is always busy constructing a model of reality, a guiding set of values and twistings of the normative as we live into and become curious about new territories in our life and how they may fit the larger patterns that identify us.
- A myth reveals that what I believe about myself and the world will influence what I believe to be true and what false.

A friend of mine in Akron, Ohio, a former myth student, has developed a non-profit organization working with young black male youths in that city and in Copley, Ohio. He calls it Alchemy, Inc. I have gone to his gatherings three times to work with Kwame Scruggs and his young men. At one of the gatherings, he posed to them this question: What are the two most important days in your life? He lets them play with possible answers. A couple of the young men rightly responded that it was the day they were born. Kwame's answers are below.

1. The day you were born.
2. The day you discover why.[1]

The first question touches on matters of biology; the second on matters of mythology. Our personal myths push us to ask why we are here and what we have decided to serve during this precious time. But one must be awake to hear these questions.

Our personal myth is also the energy and the template we use to transform the multiple events that happen to us daily—with at first-glance seeming to have little relation to one another—into a coherent story. In the process of remembering them, we shape these past events into meaningful memories; that is what a personal myth offers us: a coherent narrative out of the raw data of daily events. Things happen to us. They don't truly mean much of anything until reflected upon, so the myth we are in conjures their meaning by shaping them from their raw to their cooked state. Without this crucial myth-making act of imagination, our lives will generally feel scattered, disconnected, even alien to us. Sometimes we may find ourselves admitting: "I don't feel like myself today." Or "I don't know what I'm doing here." These observations signal moments of mythic awareness that something is out of place.

Let's travel now in the time left, into the poetic landscape of Epic literature.

Epic Literature

This all-inclusive literary genre is an aesthetic form of remembrance. Epics remember the past of a people, not just an individual. They reveal to us patterns of human thought and action:

- Whoever the epic hero is, that person carries the values, beliefs, and aspirations of an entire people they represent.
- So the epic imagination is enormous and particular simultaneously, as I will show by using a few illustrations in *From War to Wonder: Recovering Your Personal Myth Through Homer's* Odyssey.
- Epics carry the values, beliefs, prejudices and aspirations of a people in what they have chosen to remember, often in ritual, as well as what they have decided collectively or been coerced into forgetting. The construction of an epic poem is a rich ritual process of creating a story that reveals what a people believes in, what they deny and deflect and what they choose to forget.
- Epics bring to the fore what is most acutely emulated, scoop these emulations from the past, through the present

and then project forward as their collective destiny. Epics involve then the grand sweep of time itself while also affording glimpses of the mysterious and transcendent.

- Epics bring forth the best and most vital and vibrant elements of a culture or civilization's myth while discarding those shards that no longer serve their functional relationship with the world.

A collective myth reveals itself in other ways as well. In order to discern the myth that a people holds sacred and in high regard, note what national holidays they celebrate, what speeches are given, what the state of the country is in as well as what it aspires to, and you will sense what forces and persuasions drive the national mythology. Think, for instance in our country, of Armistice Day, Labor Day, Veterans Day, MLK Day, Memorial Day, Christmas Day, Easter Sunday, the State of the Union Speech; these are some of many others that are important markers.

Another country's myth might run bulls through the streets or have a horse race in an ancient arena in Siena, Italy or Athens, Greece. What a country closes its banks and federal buildings in remembrance of indicates clearly another pocket in which its prevailing myth resides. What we memorialize is precisely what we mythologize. These national days of remembrance in memory also outline that people's destiny, what they strive for, and which designates what they value as guiding principles. Such is the multi-colored fabric of epic. They are as unique as the national flag of a country which symbolically reveals something of great value woven into their national identity.

In the landscape of epic, some great achievement is often the point of the remembrance. The epic, then, is not just concerned with the destiny of one figure; rather, it creates an entire cosmos, that is, a state of order and coherence, even purpose, that must be grasped imaginatively by the reader or listener as they step into that cosmic landscape to experience the action as a mirror of what resides within the heart of the participants. My mentor, Louise Cowan, has written elegantly of these characteristics in her introductory essay, "Epic as Cosmopoiesis" in *The Epic Cosmos*.

With each epic, even each literary work, we ask: what does this classic work in print, film, painting or music ask me to contemplate and become more conscious of, and what *way* or *angle of vision* does it encourage me to assume as I think about it? Next, what does it evoke in me? And knowing that whatever way—it will be filtered and screened selectively through the myth that I am living *by means of.*

I hope the following quote helps to clarify the above point: "A myth can make a cow sacred in one culture and a hamburger patty in another," as mythologist Sam Keen expresses it in his *Your Mythic Journey* (xi). The former feeds the soul; that latter feeds the body. Same animal (literal); two contrasting myths to give it meaning (figural).

We refer to this form of interpretation as Hermeneutics, namely, the art of interpreting, named after the god Hermes, the messenger god carrying notes from Olympus to us mortals; he is also the trickster god, the thief, the clever rogue and the leader of souls into the underworld after death.

So let's name some epics:

- The Sumerian epics *Gilgamesh* and *Inanna*
- *Don Quixote*
- *The Iliad*
- *The Odyssey*
- *The Aeneid*
- *The Divine Comedy*
- *Paradise Lost*
- *Moby-Dick*
- *Beloved*
- *Go Down, Moses*
- *The Mahabharata*
- *The Ramayana*
- *The Song of Igor*
- *War and Peace*
- *Gone with the Wind*
- *Ulysses*
- *The Wasteland*
- *Woman Warrior*
- *House Made of Dawn*
- *Black Elk Speaks*
- *Ceremony*

In film:

- *Braveheart*
- *1917*
- *Frozen II*
- *The Star Wars* series, with the more current film featuring Rey, a woman as epic hero replacing Luke Skywalker
- *Wonder Woman*
- *Just Mercy*
- *The Star Trek* series
- *Who Will Write Our History?*

This last entry deserves a bit of commentary. When the Nazi regime moved into Poland in 1939, they began to herd the Jewish population of the city of Warsaw into what would be designated the Warsaw Ghetto. As their incarceration intensified, some Jewish members of the Ghetto realized that their own story would certainly be eclipsed by the Nazi's version of them, unless they acted in secret to preserve their stories, and with them, their collective identity. They began, under the leadership of Emanuel Ringelblum, to write out or draw, then consolidate their current experiences, sufferings, deprivations and bravery. Several heroic Jews agreed to secretly gather these stories at prescribed intervals from various quarters of the city: drawings, poems and artifacts from those confined to the Ghetto, and deliver them to the basement of one of the buildings in the city. There they were arranged, boxed and placed into a storage area beneath the basement floor that was dug out for the express purpose of guaranteeing their preservation.

Then, in 1944 the Nazis set fire to the Warsaw Ghetto, in part to burn out all the Jews hiding in the buildings; moreover, the regime also hoped to destroy the evidence of their own involvement in the assassination of so many of the Jewish population, to erase it from cultural memory. Later, the remaining Jews who knew of this project began to study maps of the city to locate the rubble of the building, under which survived, they prayed, the buried boxes preserving the preserved narratives of the Jewish people.

They found from maps the precise building whose basement floor was dug up to bury the boxes. A woman who was part of the initial plan to gather these pieces of her people's history, Rachel Auerbach, returned there, to have the building's rubble removed. Miraculously, down below the basement was a dug-out space in which the boxes were stored, still intact. In them, as we watch the documentary, we see their contents: charcoal drawings, letters, testaments, stories of pain, deprivation, hope and heroism. Unfortunately, another cache of boxes was never recovered.

In these six boxes rested their history, their identity, their collective aspirations and fears, their determinations to continue to live and flourish after the war. In short, in these boxes are their individual and collective mythologies, *their* narratives, not the ones the Nazis would have eminently preferred to tell the world in order to erase the identity of all those who suffered the torments of the Ghetto and who died in the camps throughout Poland. That is the stuff of epic: telling the story of an entire people so their values, aspirations, dreams, sufferings and destinies could continue to live in the world as emblems of heroism for others. To extend this narrative into our own lives: if we don't tell our story, we each must eventually recognize, someone else will tell our story for us; it will then no longer be our story but the narrative others have chosen as our legacy, right or wrong, direct or distorted. No greater theft can befall an individual than to have their story confiscated and someone else's put in its place. Our storied selves are indeed our identity selves.

But to lead into the part of my book that I want to concentrate on, I must mention what lies behind world epics generally. The Quest, the Call to Adventure, the impulse or vocation to leave the safety of what is familiar, to venture into the unknown, the unforeseen, the dangerous and ambiguous pockets of life, and there, perhaps frequently, to confront the dragons of one's own fears, uncertainties and limitations. Such a quest also has as its aim to reclaim the joys, the achievements, the accomplishments, the moments of courage that also define each of us. It requires courage, a certain steadfastness and humility, to risk moving towards what cannot be seen or foreseen.

Odysseus is a fine representative of the epic hero seeking his homeland and his home while his steadfast and heroic wife Penelope holds the raucous suitors at bay so that Odysseus has a home to return to. Their son Telemachos, now a young man gaining a foothold in his own authority, contributes to his father's safe return by sustaining the household in the face of adversaries whose appetites threaten to devour the entire *oikos,* or household.

After battling side-by-side with other Achaeans for ten years to defeat the Trojans, the central story in Homer's other epic, the *Iliad,* Odysseus begins his long journey home with his men and ships. He will spend ten years struggling to reach his homeland, his *nostos,* in Greek, but he is repeatedly delayed, deflected, detained and deferred by forces both mortal and immortal. Who has not felt his frustrations in moments of one's own life journey?

The epic begins with the first four books of the twenty-four that comprise this epic of homecoming; the early books feature the development of the now twenty-year-old Telemachos—someone about the age of many of you in the room who also may have recently left home to attend school at this University. For Telemachos is guided by the goddess Athene, daughter of Zeus, who mentors him by suggesting he now leave home and, with her guidance, discover his father's history and perhaps his destiny. She invites the young hero into the realm of stories; the more Telemachos hears episodes of his father, the more he will begin to know him and, in the process, know himself more deeply.

My intention in writing the book was not to repeat the story, which is also true of books following the same pattern in two other epics, Day-*to-Day Dante: Exploring Personal Myth Through the Divine Comedy* and *Our Daily Breach: Exploring Your Personal Myth through Herman Melville's Moby-Dick.* The structure of all three books is the same: 1) to situate some dozen or fewer lines from the epic in 365 installments, one for each day of the year; 2) to offer a one paragraph summary of what is taking place at that moment in the plot; 3) to offer a paragraph which meditates on just how that passage may have direct relevance to our lives today; 4) to prescribe a "Writing Meditation" at the bottom of each page for the reader to engage by connecting the passage and the meditation to their own specific story in order to highlight something important about their own evolving identity, their own personal myth.

Thus, there exists an interactive intention in all three books. Our focus, however, is on *From War to Wonder.* So let's look at a few examples. Nothing I say is in anyway complete; rather, like the epics themselves in their rich complexity, they are meant to evoke some response in you, which of course may be edited over time. Otherwise, without our active participation, the epic remains incomplete, unfinished, awaiting a response from us, the reader-journeyers that will aid in the classic's completion, a closing of the circle, so to speak, by having you, the reader-journeyer add something to the epic's evolving meaning.

The following are a handful of passages that we can look at closely and then invite your response to whatever in the passage evoked something in you about your own life.

January 10: Athene invites Telemachos to be instructed. She instructs him what to do.

January 11: Beginning the process of stepping into his own authority is the result of being called, being called *out*, being called *to* by a divine voice.

January 13: Telemachos begins to speak out of his own authority. He frightens the suitors devouring his family's household, who suddenly detect a radical change in him.

January 26: Telemachos hears the call; he decides to respond to it, to yield to it. He informs his nurse, Eurycleia that he is leaving home for the first time, to venture into the world in search of his father as well as the stories being told about him.

January 29: He accepts and reveres his mentor, his guide; he cannot go it alone. He needs and yearns for divine assistance given to him as a precious gift. Mentors in our lives are divine gifts to aid us in our venture.

February 2: Athene instructs him when they reach the home of Nestor of Pylos that there is no need to be modest. Time to speak up, she says. The act of learning includes learning to speak, to express yourself in public and to sense the sacredness of your own authority.

You have been a superb group to be with this afternoon. I do hope to see you again.

Works Cited

Cowan, Louise. "Epic as Cosmopoiesis." *The Epic Cosmos,* edited by
    Larry Allums. General editor, Louise Cowan. The Dallas Institute
    Publications, 1992, pp 1-26.
Keen, Sam and Anne Valley-Fox. *Your Mythic Journey: Finding Meaning
    in Your Life through Writing and Storytelling.* Jeremy
    Tarcher/Putnam, 1989.

Further Reading

Olney, James. *Memory and Narrative: The Weave of Life-Writing.* U of
    Chicago P, 1998.
Randall, William Lowell. *The Stories We Are: An Essay on Self-Creation.*
    U of Toronto P, 1995.

---

[1] Attributed to Mark Twain.

9

CREATIVITY'S HUNGER[*]

The Jungian analyst Linda Schierse Leonard reminds us in her fine study, *The Call to Create: Celebrating Acts of Imagination*, that the word *create,* from the Latin, *creare*, means to originate, to cause to exist, to bring about; it also carries the meanings of to organize, to found, to originate, to generate, to procreate and to compose. I guess then something is as simple and difficult as to "keep one's composure" is itself a creative act. I also agree with her assessment that "without expressing the creative spark in us, we are less than fully human" (4).

Not only is creativity, to my mind, a religious and a spiritual experience (the terms are not synonyms), it is also a response to a deep hunger. So, let me begin there. Not many mornings ago, as I settled into my easy chair in my study at 4:30 a.m. (I slept in; usually I am in there lighting a candle and settling down with a cup of coffee, at 4:00 a.m.), I thought of what hunger is within me that prompts a need to be nourished by the spirit of creativity. It must be made manifested, incarnated in some ways that can be shared. Perhaps a yearning for community, for sharing what one has cultivated and harvested is behind it, driving it down and in, then out.

In a more recent book that I was fortunate enough to be asked to co-author with two colleagues, *Deep Creativity: Seven Ways to Spark Your Creative Spirit,* Debora Anne Quibell writes: "The relationship with the muse is never one-sided or simple. You have to be open to her seduction, receptive to her appearance, and pleasing to entice her to

[*] Presented to the Unitarian Universalists of New Braunfels, May 26, 2019.

return. It is, I would dare say, a two-way seduction" (107). Her words are chosen carefully: *open, receptive* and *pleasing,* words that may summon, even seduce the muse(s) to be present when you are open to the vistas that they may reveal, as happens to me in the early hours of each morning. In the darkness and silence, the solitude and silkiness of my study with one candle and a small lamp burning, I am open and receptive. I have learned that creativity does not like an abundance of light unless it comes from within. More friendly, low wattage illumination is a preferable atmosphere for the shadowy muses to enter. If I could harness the light of a full moon and plug it into my study, that light would be optimum.

The following is what emerged, of their own accord, from such a meditation on creativity. Here is something else: a creative life cannot be forced, coerced or "handled." It is a gift that appears if one is deemed open enough to let go of the command center in one's soul. Letting *go* is prelude to letting *up,* then letting *in* what is hungry to enter.

Creativity is, as Leonard intuits, a calling; it is vocative, a voice from within the deeper self that slices through practicality, daily habits and routines to announce itself. The call to create resides in a deep hunger that permeates and provokes every cell of our bodies. It excites the desire for its own food groups, with specific nutrients attached to each one. Another writer, Aimee Bender, also has her eye on nutrition when she writes on memorizing a particularly moving poem by Wallace Stevens: "I think we're biologically impacted by language. It can be deeply, deeply nourishing. And I don't mean that as a metaphor. It can feel like something cellular gets fed" (*Light the Dark* 3).

I use **ours** above because I do not think that what follows is particular to me alone. I believe that one of the most known calls to create begins Herman Melville's epic journey, *Moby-Dick* when the narrator begins with the oft-quoted line: "Call me Ishmael" (3). Now if you say that line aloud, you suddenly become Ishmael, the one who wishes to be called. His name means "God shall hear." "Call me" is what each of us yearns for in a creative moment: to be called to adventure. It is as well, in Leonard's title above, *The Call to Create.* What follows is my sense of this hunger to create, which I hope you add to.

Creativity is

- A hunger to engage life more deeply than our busy everyday realities encourage or allow room for.
- A hunger to relate more deeply with ourselves, others and life itself; such a hunger can and does heal a divorce or a lengthy separation we have imposed on ourselves or had done for us and to us. So, this hunger is a desire to reconcile.
- A hunger for adventure: to enter the woods where there is no path to follow, or its outlines are so shady and opaque; then one knows she is on her path, not someone else's.
- A hunger to leave a trace in the form of some markers that affirm we were present on this earth, that we participated in life, and that we changed it for the better in some way.
- But—this hunger can also breed a creativity that destroys, that annihilates, that damages people, things, ideas, institutions and all those afflicted by it. This hunger is often fueled by desperation, isolation, intoxication, fed by erroneous beliefs, even ideologies—a kind of Molotov cocktail in the mind ready to be lit, its wick the emblem of wickedness. But the impulse arises from the same hunger I am contemplating here. Denying its shadow would be naïve.
- A hunger to transcend our understanding of who we are with our limitations, abbreviations, emendations, our narrowness, our self-incarcerations, and to connect with a realm of invisible presences that are eternally present to provoke us into a fuller awareness. It is an expression of awakening.
- A hunger for communion and for community to incarnate our imagination in order to connect with a larger collective myth that carries us beyond our personal set of mythic structures to allow more in.
- A hunger to risk something, to step out of our current cultural obsessions with safety and security, which can jail us from life more than it encourages participation in love;

it is to risk feeling the essential groundlessness of our lives as it passes more swiftly as we grow into our full identity. In short, to live within and celebrate our vulnerabilities.

- A hunger to feel in our bones a deeper courage—life lived from within the heart—and to feel the hearth fire of ourselves burning in the heated glow of the coals of our unlived potentials. It taps those places we are yet to live out.

- A hunger to awaken, to become more conscious, more aware, of what our place in the cosmos is and for, and what our purpose in life truly involves.

- A hunger to give a coherent shape and order to what may feel at times like a series of disconnected days and an endless string of unrelated events without linkage, and more darkly, without purpose or overarching meaning, which is bedrock for our personal myth.

- A hunger to break free from the shackles of our own often self-imposed conventional limitations, definitions and descriptions of what and who we are.

- A hunger to feel at times, or often, or even occasionally what it is like to live closer to our full capacity, to push against all those "I can't" s that envelop us in a stamped, self-admonishing envelope mailed to ourselves, often in an overnight Fed Ex packet that arrives weekly as a reminder.

- A hunger to live outside of the at-times totalitarian control of our ego, with all its busy labelling, and inside a more functional relationship with our Self, the place and purpose of our higher and deeper calling.

- A hunger to kick up the dust or to kick through the wall of our conventional story lines, the relentless narratives that more often than not, constrict, restrict, and choke the flow of our vital life spirit that often repeats the message:

- "Don't you dare"// "Don't risk it"// "It's not safe"// and the big white whale of doom: "You might fail."

- A hunger, paradoxically, to accept our incapacities, as does Jung in *The Red Book,* by slaying the heroic in us that can become a bigger hindrance in the long run than any inability we might ferret out.

- A hunger for ritual, for incarnating our thoughts, insights, revelations or understandings into a coherent form, for giving it integrity and for proposing it tangibly to the world.

- A hunger for sacrifice, for giving up something that has outlived its shelf life in order to make room for what has been birthed into being or wants to be, for relinquishing, for absenting our life of something that no longer serves us.

- A process of eliminating what we no longer need. Another way of expressing this idea is that allowing certain parts of ourselves to disintegrate is at the same moment a benign occasion to integrate what has remained loose ends in our lives, wayward or rogue threads that have resisted being woven into the larger fabric of our fiction. Their resistance to be integrated may be a signal of its supreme value.

- A hunger for the bliss that lies in the deepest recesses of us that we rarely tap into, much less even reach and connect with.

- A moment of transformation; we long for these moments of conversion but often seek them in the world rather than within the terrain of our own mystery, our own miracle of becoming.

- To follow one's bliss, as Joseph Campbell made public knowledge. It involves accepting the pain and the challenge, the difficulties that form blisters on our soul as part of the price tag, a necessity in the realization of one's deeper sense of why one is on this earth. Bliss may not be a joy ride but it is an authentic deployment of who we are and what our purpose is.

- A hunger to be in contact with what Jung described as the collective unconscious, from which so much creativity emanates. "A new consciousness occurs," he writes, "when suddenly there is a flash of insight between two apparently disconnected and widely separated ideas and this has the effect of releasing a latent tension" (*CW* 17, par. 207).

- A hunger for the journey into opposites, into contradictions, and beyond that to paradox, where the act of creation may occasion a reconciliation of them through a joining, a unifying of what was split and gnaws away at one's sense of wholeness and unity.
- To live a creative life is to explore and engage one's level of a coherent life, for creativity and coherence are blood brothers and sisters and both must be honored and extolled. Perhaps then where our life coheres is where the force of creativity creates its richest habitation.

Works Cited

Fassler, Joe, editor. *Light the Dark: Writers on Creativity, Inspiration, and the Artistic Process.* Penguin Books, 2017.

Jung, C.G. *The Development of Personality.* Vol. 17. Translated by R.F. C. Hull. Sir Herbert Read, Michael Fordham, et.al, editors, translated by R.F.C. Hull. *The Collected Works of C.G. Jung,* Princeton UP, 1981.

Leonard, Linda Schierse. *The Call to Create: Celebrating Acts of Imagination.* Harmony Books, 2000.

Melville, Herman. *Moby-Dick, or, The Whale.* Easton Press, 1977.

Quibell, Deborah Anne, Jennifer Leigh Selig and Dennis Patrick Slattery. *Deep Creativity: Seven Ways to Spark Your Creative Spirit.* Shambhala Publications, 2019.

Further Reading

Bohm, David and F. David Peat. *Science, Order, and Creativity.* 2nd edition. Routledge, 2000.

---. *On Creativity.* Routledge, 1996.

---. *Wholeness and the Implicate Order.* Routledge, 1980.

Chodron, Pema. *The Wisdom of No Escape and the Path of Loving Kindness.* Shambhala Publications, 2001.

Singer, Thomas, editor. *The Vision Thing: Myth, Politics and Psyche in the World.* Routledge, 2000.

Slattery, Dennis Patrick. *Our Daily Breach: Exploring Your Personal Myth Through Herman Melville's Moby-Dick*. Fisher King Press, 2015.

---. *Bridge Work: Essays on Mythology, Literature and Psychology*. Mandorla Books, 2015.

10

ON CREATIVITY: A MEMOIR PROJECT[*]

In any war story, but especially a true one, it's difficult to separate what happened from what seemed to happen. What seems to happen becomes its own happening and has to be told that way.

~Tim O'Brien, *The Things They Carried,* 71

A story that is interpreted for me still needs to be interpreted by *me, by what I do* with *it—and what it does with me.*

~David R. Loy, *The World is Made of Stories,* 27

Some Reflections and an Invitation

If we had more time together, we would work on what appears below as a group. Nonetheless, I hope you accept the invitation to creatively explore your own personal myth. Its dimensions are embedded in your life narrative, regardless of your age. One is never too old or too young to begin this exploration. What I suggest below is one of many ways to leave a legacy of your life as **you** imagine it, not as it is imagined and told by others. Relating one's own life is one of the most treasured legacies we can leave in the world for others to enjoy.

---

[*] Presented to The Jung Society of Utah, November 16, 2018.

Unfortunately, not many leave a written legacy of what they found life-altering, life-transforming and life-enhancing in their pilgrimage through their world. My own parents wrote nothing down to leave to us and to their grandchildren, and now, to their great grandchildren. I do not want to follow in that tradition. I do recall as a young boy my mother having me sit down with her because she wanted to show me a host of photographs that lay quietly in a cardboard box. Among them were black and white photos of relatives, many of whom were still living, in Ireland. I was not interested, so self-absorbed was I with my tiny frame of reference on *my* world. Looking now through a rear-view mirror, I wish I had been able to record her stories through the photos she used to ignite her memory. My enormous loss. My siblings' enormous loss as well. We have carried that amnesia through our adult lives.

I would have loved to read about their own image of their lives, what they aspired to and dreamed about, what they believed they did and did not live, what part of life remained unfulfilled but was itself part of their life's trajectory, if not its conclusion. I would have enjoyed witnessing what they believed gave each of their lives a coherence that was unique to them, as well as what obstacles stood in their way to perhaps achievements that would have surprised themselves most of all. I would have listened differently then, to notice what identity emerged slowly, from each told narrative, that comprised and textured their unique time on earth. I would have been a true relative of them by means of their stories. And what did they know, if anything, about who I actually was?

So, with the above as a frame of reference, here is what I propose and encourage you to pursue. Yes, I know, writing takes discipline, a schedule, a fierce intention that does not waver; however, as a life-long writer, I have found that writing is one of the most creative ways of discovering what we truly think, believe in, feel inadequate about, sense joy in, what we struggle after and achieve. It also occasions moments of immense courage to note and give form to where we fell short, refused callings, hovered over a thought or a plan for a future, but never really committed to it. Where we falter in life are places and moments where we reach our edge, touch our soft, vulnerable places, our limits, and often pull back, instead of allowing a free-fall into the unknown and unexpected. Remembering may be one rich way at our fingertips of moving into an uncharted future by means of our histories, as paradoxical as that may seem. Here is the chart for you to follow, amend, edit and make your own. Don't be too rigid here, just authentic:

- Give some initial thought to and then write down ten (10) sentences. Let each one signify an important event in your life, a cross-roads, a major turn; let it include events that shaped and formed you, that transformed you and may have led you to a fuller life in remembering them through writing.
- The above comprises the ten chapters of your life. Of course, you could name more, but for the boundaries of this project, ten is sufficient.
- Next, order them, but not necessarily by chronology but by their psychic and emotional importance, by the amount of energy they carry for you even now and by their effect on you to this day. Chronology lists events as they happened in sequence; I am suggesting that you list them according to mythic time, to importance, valence, power in shaping your narrative life.
- Yes, you can order them chronologically, but I ask that you consider the above point and use a different frame of reference if you think doing so would give a fuller and more mythically accurate version of your identity.
- Keep your imagination attuned to where incidents of transformation entered your life. We can often see them most clearly in imagination's rear-view mirror; sometimes that mirror is concave or convex in structure. Events have the capacity and tendency to ripen over time, both into greater or lesser significance. What you may have remembered a dozen years ago as crucially important might not even make the top ten cut as you remember it today.
- If it is helpful, choose an audience you want to address. I would, for instance choose my three granddaughters, McKenzie (19), Eleanor (7) and Siena (3). Or I might choose our two sons, Matt (47) and Steve (42).

As you consider the above, I want to suggest possible arenas, fields, or categories that might aid you in becoming more fully aware of options in the construction of your precious ten sentences or phrases.

- Moments of coming to or recognizing your strongest beliefs. Let one or two suffice here.
- Moments of strongest disillusionments.
- Moments of loss.
- Moments of unlived (to date) designs.
- Moments of greatest achievements.
- Moments of a dream or two that has been with you for years, perhaps repeats itself periodically or that you recorded at one point because of its dramatic effect on you.
- Moments of reading something that changed you, or a film you saw and return to or a play that attracted you on a deep level of awareness. Even one line of a poem has the capacity to alter your consciousness.
- Moments of crossroads, turning points, that formed a crux in the direction of your life.
- Moments of threshold crossings where you sensed your life moving out of one stage into another. Note here as well if there was present a threshold guardian that either blocked your way or facilitated your crossing.
- Moments of deepest friendship, love for another or others.
- Moments of contributing to the larger world.
- Moments of realizing what you will die not having done.
- Moments of prideful pursuits.
- Moments of failure, falling short, falling down, falling away.
- Moments of greatest resilience.
- Moments of remarkable recovery.
- Moments where your memory is gappy; in this instance fill in the gaps by making the story up. The make-believe part of your story is also a valid segment of your history and fills out another component of your identity.
- Moments when one or two of your deepest and current assumptions were formed.

- Moments when one of your deepest assumptions was shattered.
- Moments in which you came across a poem, a quote, a saying, that you felt encompassed something of great value in and for you. Cite them.
- Moments when you realized with great joy why you were put on this earth.
- You may add to this list, but that is sufficient for now to get you going.

Write ten (10) pages on each of the sentences you have chosen to give your life its important moments and events. So, a total of 100 pages.

Write it out in cursive first in a journal or other vehicle that attracts you and is worthy of your narrative as its first container. Cursive writing will slow you down and allow more meditative responses to what you are crafting.

Keep a little spiral notebook, one that fits in your pocket. Once you activate your past in writing, the imagination will keep working it whether you are ready to write or not. You do not want to miss these fleeting instances of insight, so be prepared. Your sentences may in fact change; you may find yourself deleting some and replacing them with others. If this process is truly organic, which I think it will be for you, then be open and prepared for change-ups in what has been in fact important. Toni Morrison, author of many novels, including the award-winning *Beloved*, said in an interview: "something happens in your life on Thursday that seems trivial, insignificant; then ten, twenty years later, you look back and see it now as a major turning point in your life." Recall that the word "trivial" stems from "tri-via," three roads. Where they meet is often a moment of great change, even if we do not see it clearly in the moment.

Avoid the tendency to "conceptualize" your life, making it an abstraction rather than an enfleshed living reality. You are seeking the storyline that has shaped you and formed your identity. Now in writing about it, you are giving it form in order to comprehend its large and small contours, patterns and even purposes. No wonder that as we get older and a bit more ripened, we look back more often than forward in order to comprehend the narrative we have been creating and being created by.

But even that is not enough. I think a deeper reality begins to emerge on reflective remembering: we begin to notice the deep psychic and emotional, even spiritual patterns that have guided us, giving our lives purpose, momentum and memorableness; these patterns may in part be chosen consciously by us, but I think something more is at work. Our destiny is apparent in the patterns that unfold us into the world and then spiral back to shape our interior life.

These same patterns may align themselves and become conscious through moments of inspiration. I have written elsewhere: "Being inspired can come at us in the oddest moments. Jotting at least a few words down is enough to recall what began to brew in me in those instants that are as ephemeral as a passing cloud" ("Origin and Originality: What Spurs Us to Create?" 308). Patterns inspirit our lives, give them texture and resilience. Run amuck, patterns of thought and behavior can incarcerate us in a prison whose bars were constructed by us, one at a time over years, even decades. Recognizing any of our life patterns signals moments of awakening.

Do not worry too much about absolute accuracy. Pay more attention to the experience's intensity and veracity and the way they gain emotional presence as you recall them. Accept at the outset that you, like any of us, are part fact, part fiction, part conjectures and assumptions, fictions, fantasies, paradoxes, forgeries and fabrications. Listen to Tim O'Brien's reflection on memory from his popular work on the Vietnam War, *The Things They Carried*: "Forty-three years old, and the war occurred half a lifetime ago, and yet the remembering makes it now. And sometimes remembering will lead to a story, which makes it forever. That's what stories are for" (38). As we remember, we story, and those stories are not exclusively anchored in the past; they also point us to our future.

As to fabri-creations, look at how you are dressed right now. It is less a fashion statement than it is a fiction statement, even a mythic statement, of your imagined self, your continually unfolding identity. There is value in knowing where the lines are drawn in your life regarding the above categories and qualities. The more particular you can be in your remembrances that offer a myriad of detail, the more you will be engaging everyone's story—by analogy: through remembrance, through likeness, through accord, because you will have tapped into some of the universal patterns that shape each of us. When he spoke of our mythic dimensions, Joseph Campbell would include innate tendencies in each of us that reveal patterns by which our lives are lived, if not loved.

If you trust this process, your story will take on both width and depth in its arrangement, its structure, as well as its content. Out of such a confluence will arise a dramatic coherence, a sense of a patterned wholeness which is the center of who you are. I also believe we can be dramatically or subtly awakened through our remembrances, whether they *in fact* unfolded in just that way historically.

Your story's content will provoke in readers a context by which they can discern/recall substances of their own story. Therefore, you owe it to yourself and others not to leave this world without marking a trace of your life told and fixed in words, subject always of course, to change in the form of edits and revisions as you remember both more and differently. If you are gifted with the ability to draw or paint, you might want to illustrate a couple of the stories you tell, or even include a precious photo that remembers that time with you.

When finished, ask: Do I discern any patterns

Of thought
Of behavior
Of fantasy
Of dreams
Of desires

as well as other categories that reveal the multi-colored threads of my myth?

Writing initially in cursive, not with a computer, is a rich method to remember and to forge relationships with other aspects of your life; cursive writing slows the entire process down and may even allow for a deeper form of recollection. Revising when you have completed the one hundred pages is also part of this organic quality of a life recorded in stories and a coherent identity forged through them.

When you have finished writing it out and then, if you wish, typing it up, find an attractive binder or container for it. Make several copies. Give them away and enjoy allowing yourself to live in the world in this beautiful format.

In closing, giving the above a chance may be seen by you at the time or years later, as one of the most creative acts you have engaged. You will be surprised at what you have created; your family and friends will be grateful to you for remembering yourself into their present and future and then into generations after them.

Works Cited

Loy, David R. *The World is Made of Stories*. Wisdom Publications, 2010.

Morrison. Toni. *Profile of a Writer*. Public Media Home Vision, 1987. Cassette tape.

O'Brien, Tim. *The Things They Carried*. Houghton Mifflin, 1990.

Slattery, Dennis Patrick. "Origin and Originality." In Deborah Anne Quibell, Jennifer Leigh Selig, et al. *Deep Creativity: Seven Ways to Spark Your Creative Spirit*. Shambhala Publications, 2019, pp. 308-18.

Further Reading

Bradt, Kevin M., SJ. *Story as a Way of Knowing*. Sheed and Ward, 1997.

Conforti, Michael. *Field, Form, and Fate: Patterns in Mind, Nature, and Psyche*. Revised edition. Spring Journal Books, 2003.

Hollis, James. *Finding Meaning in the Second Half of Life*. Gotham Books, 2005.

McAdams, Dan P. *The Stories We Live By: Personal Myths and the Making of the Self*. Guilford Press, 1993.

Miller, J. Hillis. *Ariadne's Thread: Story Lines*. Yale UP, 1992.

Punter, David. *Metaphor*. The New Critical Idiom. Routledge, 2007.

Spence. Donald P. *Narrative Truth and Historical Truth: Meaning and Interpretation in Psychoanalysis*. W.W. Norton, 1982.

11

THE POWER OF BEARING WITNESS

Another Texas treasure that does not seem to be well known is the San Antonio Jewish Community Center located at Northwest Military and Wurzbach Roads. It is more than a center; it is a small campus, complete with an elementary school, athletic facilities, a swimming pool, a host of conferences and talks as well as a noteworthy Holocaust Museum.

On Friday, February 17th, 2017 I found my way to this elegant set of buildings to meet a friend, Dr. Roger Barnes, who as part of his new course on the Holocaust in the University of Incarnate Word's Sociology program, invited his students to the Museum this morning for several reasons. He had organized a historical talk with a docent, Mr. Len King, a tour offered by Director of Programs, Matthew Faulkner, and a special guest speaker, Ms. Anna Weisz Rado, a Holocaust survivor of the Auschwitz concentration camp. Students from Dr. Lisa Lockhart's psychology class also attended, as did English faculty member, Dr. Emily Clark.

For the first 45 minutes students, their parents and visiting faculty were encouraged to wander through the round conference room whose walls were covered with photos and words from both prisoners as well as Nazi officers regarding the internment camps in Germany. One large elegant display highlighted the scrolled Torah, along with a prayer shawl and other elements of ritual reading. Other rooms as well as the main lecture hall were filled with material depicting life in the camps. In one room glasses cases contained a broken spoon as well as a porcelain conductor guide for electric wiring that surrounded each concentration camp. Photographs showed prisoners in their tiny bunks; in one of them a very young Elie Wiesel peers out between two prisoners. The lecture hall was packed, but as students and faculty read and examined the material, a profound silence, broken only by a few muted conversations, embraced the group.

When the presentations began, we listened to Len's historical framing of the Third Reich, beginning with WW I and extending into WW II. He used the photos lining the circular walls to guide his presentation; that he paused periodically to ask if the students had questions was helpful. The amount of material covered needed periodic reprieves from the details of the horrors perpetrated on the innocent. It could easily become overwhelming. All of the students were respectful and completely absorbed in the presentation. Len informed us that over 11 million people died in WW II; of that number, 6.5 million were Jews. More than 1.5 million of those executed were children under 11 years of age. Other groups included gypsies, Catholics, Protestants and others who were deemed marginal or undesirable members of society, in accordance with Hitler's brutal assessment of humanity that did not measure up to his purity fantasies.

When Len finished, Matthew introduced the guest speaker, Ms. Anna Wiesz Rado, whose recounting of her survival at Auschwitz absorbed all of us. Anna speaks frequently to a variety of groups about her and her family's experience; part of her intention is to keep in our collective memory what historical horror comprised the Nazis' desire to exterminate an entire people. But her story was less about victimhood of suffering and terrible deaths of millions than it was about hope, forgiveness and courage, as well as the trauma and possible subsequent healing that accompanies remembering and expressing that haunting past. At the end of her talk she wanted us to understand: "If you don't give up and you believe in God, you can get over it," referring to the lingering realities that can consume any member of such a shocking period in their lives, including the loss of family members, which in many cases did occur within minutes of a family arriving at a camp.

Anna will be 86 on February 26th, 2017. She was born in Hungary in a small village that included 300 Jews. At the time of the liberation of the camps in 1945, and when she made her journey back to the place of her birth, only 15 Jews from her village had survived, including her brother and sister. The Germans initially invaded Hungary in 1939. Anna and all other Jews were required from that time forward to wear the yellow star sewn and displayed on their clothing. She related how when she returned to school wearing the star, all the young people whose friendships she had enjoyed now turned on and bullied her and other children who bore the yellow star; shortly thereafter, all Jews were forbidden to attend school. Later, she and her family, who were allowed only three suitcases in which to put their life's possessions, were sent some 35 miles away to a ghetto. All were thoroughly searched for hidden jewelry, which if found, was immediately confiscated.

When she was 13 years old in June of 1944, she and her family were crowded into boxcars destined for Auschwitz; at the last moment before slamming the door to the boxcar, a German soldier threw two buckets inside to be used as toilets for the dozens of people packed into a rancid and suffocating space. Anna related one of her keenest memories, which she recalled often to save her from despair. A young mother was trying to nurse her infant, but she had no breast milk because she was severely dehydrated. One of the other prisoners found in his suitcase a can of tomato paste and generously gave it to the young mother, who fed her infant the contents of the can. That incident helped Anna adhere to the idea that "there are more good people in the world than evil ones."

When the train arrived at Auschwitz, children were immediately separated from their parents; those who were old, feeble or otherwise unable to work were quickly led off to the gas chambers. There was no time or allowance for goodbyes, nor for last minute offerings of affection. For Anna, this sudden and abrupt loss of both parents was the worst pain of any that she endured in the camp and in her subsequent struggle to return home.

Twice she was saved from being executed through words of advice or twists of fate that she believes was God's plan for her: to survive to tell her story and that of others. She also escaped becoming one of hundreds of victims of Dr. Mengele, who for years conducted experiments on the inmates, which included maiming, blinding, and castrating many of them in the process under the pretense of scientific advancement.

In January of 1945 Auschwitz was liberated. In February Anna walked with others through the harsh climate and deep snow wearing wooden shoes, the only ones available to prisoners. She worked in an airplane factory until May, when she began her trek back to Budapest and then to her own village, where her brother had already returned to their former home. Years later, in 1957, because her sister lived in San Antonio, Anna immigrated with her husband to the city. Having married a cabinet maker in Hungary, she and her husband created and operated a cabinet- making business for 30 years, located at Hazel and Zarzamora streets in San Antonio.

Anna spoke for almost an hour without a note; she then responded to questions from the audience. She realized, as did we, that the number of survivors from the camps in Germany and Poland are rapidly diminishing. Soon there will be no survivors to tell their stories. But this part of history will not disappear because Anna, her sister, and many other survivors have made it their calling to speak out about their experiences in the spirit, finally, of hope. They also believe they must, through their recollections, counter the absurd assertion by various factions that the Holocaust never happened.

Dennis Patrick Slattery, Anna Weisz Rado and Roger Barnes at the Jewish Community Education Center, San Antonio, Texas February 2nd, 2017

Now, we in the audience, one of many, have heard her story and will pass it on. It is the reason for this short essay: to carry the story of courage, faith and resilience of the human spirit as well as the courageous act of forgiveness that can free the soul from the ghetto or the camp of one's own resentment and victimhood. What an honor to have been in the audience that Friday morning.

Further Reading

Anglada, Maria Angels. *The Violin of Auschwitz: A Novel.* Translated from the Catalan by Martha Tennent. Bantam Books, 2020.

Levi, Primo. *Survival in Auschwitz.* Orion Press, 1959.

Steinbacher, Sybille. *Auschwitz: A History.* Translated by Shaun Whiteside. Harper Perennial, 2005.

Who Will Write Our History? Documentary. Amazon Prime, 2019.

Wiesel, Eli. *Auschwitz.* Translated by Marion Wiesel. Hill and Wang, 2006.

PART II

ESSAYS ON
CULTURE AND PSYCHE

12

GROWTH: WHEN A MYTH NO LONGER WORKS[*]

While many "Letters to the Editor" of the *Herald-Zeitung* express a valid caution of too much development, given the immediate and longer-range necessity of conserving water in Texas, they have failed to touch the deeper question: what myth is it that compels this relentless engine of growth? Until the underlying myth that shapes the thinking of what a people value is addressed, the problem stays above ground and tends to draw to itself ways of fixing something. Fixing as solution is also a mythic structure, but it too can be little more than a limited patch work that camouflages a more adamant belief or desire.

The language of growth, development, expansion, bigger, more, enlargement, Manifest-Destiny, are all terms highlighting the same value. If myths can be categorized as both personal and collective, and if they are understood to comprise mediums of value, then they can also direct us to what is not valued and best dropped into the waste container of forgetfulness. Engineering cultural selective amnesia is itself a mythical method of deletion.

As responsible citizens, we have to be continually vigilant in order to designate and acknowledge who/what it is that makes such critical determinations. For what we are asked or persuaded to dis-remember is as powerful a force to a people's mythology as is what we are told or subtly coerced to remember, to keep in mind and to be guided by.

---

[*] "Opinion" in New Braunfels' *The Herald-Zeitung*, August 20th, 2014, p. 4.

Development, increase, expansion, enlargement have been core elements of America's values since its inception. History reveals that much has been done constructively and destructively to satisfy the appetites of these values, which are finally, insatiable. What we do as individuals and as a culture to enact, so to more firmly remember, the myths we hold closest to our identity, becomes evident in the form of rituals.

Rituals embody, incarnate and bestow integrity to what we believe to be true and necessary for our own identity, respect and growth. Rituals are embodied acts of remembrance, even enshrining values on the many altars cultures construct for just such worship. Consider, for example, ribbon-cutting ceremonies with leaders both private and public in attendance from the community, ritually smiling at their achievement of opening up a new shopping center, church, building, or park. Or a row of shovel-handling dignitaries breaking ground for everything from a new mall to a new road. The ritual is the embodied reflection of mythic values; we might want to pay attention to both.

For myths, like anything else that is organic, wear out, break down, decompose, eventually to expose their expiration date. If the myths we hold sacred prove no longer operative, constructive, helpful or that at times, given changing circumstances, require moderation, revisiting or revisioning, they will undergo change only if they are truly vibrant and organic. If they have instead calcified into some brittle form of dogmatic assertion or absolute truth or "the way things are," to the exclusion of any other options or possibilities that are more in tune with the current realities surrounding us, then the myth is akin to a cadaver than a living vibrant and organic presence.

Looking, then, below the surface of changes we wish to make as a community, such as further growth, inviting others into the state or region because of a lower tax base, so that we see the myth driving such expansion, is not only a reasonable but a moral act. Denying the mythic reality resting below the literal level of this or that policy or public action, like signing off on an increasing number of developers' permits, is both naïve and harmful to the body politics' survival.

Further Reflections on Development

We can see as never before the bristling signs of growth and change everywhere in our thriving city of New Braunfels, Texas. On percentage, we are right now the second fastest growing city in the United States. Where there were once open fields and tree-filled lots, there are now buildings for both private and public use. *Flourishing* is not too strong a term for the city of New Braunfels as it expands and fills in the gaps of our city with further housing and stores to accommodate the escalating population. But a sober sense of balance must accompany such development, which should not be an end in itself. Slogans and passive bromides to justify growth to the exclusion of any other voices, is a sign that monitoring this expansion has failed.

I am less a proponent of keeping New Braunfels "a quaint village where everyone knows everyone." We are too far along and away from that image of who we once were. I am more interested in looking at "development" as a myth that drives us and most of America generally. The general consensus is that what we hold of value identifies who we are and what we stand for.

The myth of development sits atop a larger myth—the myth of growth and consumption. Now because the word "myth" is so maligned today as meaning "untrue" or "false," an unfortunate hangover from an older myth, the myth of facts and quantification, I hesitate to use it. But I must. Contrary to popular impugning of the word, myths are expressions of the ways I as an individual or we collectively as a city or a nation, organize our awareness and define our realities according to a set of values or beliefs that we hold close to us and are even willing to fight for, and if need be—to die for. "Freedom" may be called one of our cultural myths. "Success" is another; "Efficiency" another. And yes, "Development" is another. Now the trouble with myths like "Development" is that, like a bad but relentless television commercial, it can reach extremes if left unchecked. With relentless repetition of its presence it can eventually be embraced as the only show in town. It can cloud or eradicate other ways of organizing our awareness and ways of thinking about something, by narrowing alternative perspectives.

If the myth that rests behind "Development," which is I believe a way of asserting the myth of progress, another major part of our communal and collective mindset, then perhaps we must question seriously whether that part of the myth is still a valid, or the predominantly most accepted way, of organizing our awareness so we clearly perceive what is our most perduring value. Might there be other forms of growth that do not rest on expansion of more products to be consumed, including earth space?

"Development" is itself a powerful and prevailing myth that measures, finally, how we relate to the earth, how we steward the land, and how we measure our standard of life. When we literalize the myth into new housing developments, wider streets, more access for more people, more stores to fulfill our wants without contrary energies that alert us to the value in limits, boundaries, restraint and sustainability, then we begin to sense that its prominence should be countered by articulating its shadow: seeing the stresses and fractures already prevailing on the infrastructures of our city and region, its toll on the resources of water, open space, traffic, crime rates and all the less discussed elements of our home can reveal the dark underbelly of the most revered word driving this myth: Progress. But we should ask: whose definition of Progress are we embodying here?

There is also, in addition to culture's expansion, a myth of the earth and the land, of the value of leaving the earth in large swatches to be part of the infrastructure of quality of life. "Development" as a myth implies that the earth is not good enough as she is—she must be improved, i.e. developed. "Development" and "Growth" are loaded terms, splitting the land into the dualistic positions of "undeveloped" (not good), and "developed" (good). We must question the myth first before moving into literalizing it in additional venues of filling in and filling up the limits of this beautiful land and its virtues that do not need to be developed so we can assign it supreme value. It has value in itself, if our myth will allow that perception in.

Further Reading

Bell, Catherine, editor. *Teaching Ritual.* Oxford UP, 2007.

Friedman, Leah. *The Power of Ritual: How It Can Change Our Lives.* np, 2013.

Giroux, Henry A. *The Violence of Organized Forgetting: Thinking Beyond America's Disimagination Machine.* City Lights Books, 2014.

Gallagher, Winifred. *The Power of Place: How Our Surroundings Shape Our Thoughts, Emotions, and Actions.* Poseidon Press, 1993.

Huntley, Karyl. *Real Life Rituals.* Spiritual Living Press, 2005.

Margalit, Avishai. *The Ethics of Memory*. Harvard UP, 2002.

Shapiro, Michael. *A Sense of Place: Great Travel Writers Talk About Their Craft, Lives, and Inspiration*. Travelers' Tales, 2004.

Turner, Victor. *The Ritual Process: Structure and Anti-Structure*. Aldine Transaction, 2008.

13

SPACED OUT IN WEST TEXAS*

Texas' legendary wide-open spaces took a cosmic turn recently when my wife and I headed west on a 5-day road trip to the Fort Davis Mountains and the McDonald Observatory as well as surrounding sights. From New Braunfels we opted for Highway 90 rather than I-10 to experience many of the small towns along the more scenic route. We spent the night in Sanderson and were glad we had packed a cooler; there were almost no options to eating out. The next morning, we passed through Marathon, Alpine, Marfa and up Route 17 north to Fort Davis and the magnificent Indian Lodge, about a mile above sea level and only 13 miles from the Observatory, which sits close to the highest peak in the state at 6791 feet.

The McDonald's Observatory is one of Texas' greatest treasures and site of some of the most exciting space explorations taking place on the planet. We drove up to it the same afternoon we settled into Indian Lodge; we bought tickets for the next morning's tour at 10:30. Little did we know until we arrived for the tour that we were the only ones who had signed up, so we had the very competent and entertaining docent, Kelly, to ourselves from 10:30 to 1:45. We were over the moon, so to speak, with gratitude.

Currently connected to and managed by the University of Texas at Austin Science Department, the Observatory was originally funded by banker and confederate soldier, William J. McDonald, who injected

* Originally published as "Observatory Trip Put Things In Perspective." In "Other Views" section of *The San Antonio Express-News,* December 19th, 2016. A13.

a large sum of money into UT in 1926 to finance an observatory. Today there are no less than 10 telescopes on two mountain tops: Locke and Fowlkes. We met our guide after watching a brief documentary on the history of the site and the current research of galaxies in deep space continuing today. Many of the ten scopes are used every clear night of the year, which is substantial, since this part of the United States is one of the darkest, and so more conducive to deep exploration of the stars and surrounding galaxies. Scientists from around the planet whose proposals are accepted by a committee rent time on the telescopes and stay in comfortable living quarters on the property.

Kelly then began tapping into other telescopes around the globe because cloud cover spoiled our morning and cancelled the use of scopes there. He selected a telescope in South Africa and one in Chile; the images we saw were only minutes old. He also pulled into view a telescope circling the earth that gave us magnificent photos only an hour old of explosions on the sun's surface as well as black spots that revealed cooler terrain on the sun's face. More collaboration with other countries sharing their data with one another has greatly accelerated research projects in many areas on the planet while controlling this costly research.

We were told that the kinds of research taking place at McDonalds include "the inner workings of stars, the birth of planets, the violent collisions between galaxies, as well as the fate of the universe." Heavy stuff, but with the technology improving so rapidly, these arenas, once not even thought of as too inconceivable, are now occurring from many vantage points globally.

Kelly then took a few moments to fetch a small bus, and the three of us headed up the mountain from the Frank Bash Research Center, which houses a movie theater, excellent book store and a small restaurant and extremely clean bathrooms. Our first stop was on Mount Locke and the Harlan J. Smith telescope, dedicated in 1968 and renamed in Smith's honor in 1995. It was originally built in response to the space race that heated up in the 1960s. Here the fun was about to begin.

The Smith telescope weighs 120 tons and is balanced by an equal weight. Its balance is so fine that it requires only a 1.5 horsepower motor to move it. I was given the hand-held controls with a toggle switch that could be moved in four directions; Kelly instructed me to bring the telescope, with its 107" mirror, around to line up with where the roof would open to the skies. The telescope moved smoothly and effortlessly; over 200 tons gracefully glided slowly up and toward the ceiling.

Of the two dozen or so other places on the planet with the sophistication of McDonald's, the Texas scope is in the top 10. Of course, all the equipment here is now more sophisticated than the first sky gazer to watch the heavens through a crude telescope 400 years earlier. That first astronomer was Galileo Galilei in Italy. Nonetheless, his charcoal drawings of sun spots are uncannily exact and similar in design to those photos the telescopes of today capture. Kelly's explanation of what a telescope is—a light gatherer, so that the greater in diameter its mirrors, the more light it is capable of capturing—was very helpful. The large diameter Smith telescope, as well as the newest, the Hobby-Eberly, which we visited next on the adjoining hill to see being restored and updated, are world-class scopes.

The latter, we learned, is actually a spectroscopic telescope, meaning it does not capture images so much as it splits light from an object into its component wave lengths by means of 91 identical six-sided sequential mirrors fitting together like floor tiles. Its target is objects in deep space; it pierces the light that makes up the object and its brightness, from which a trained eye can gauge its distance from the earth. Spectroscopy also reveals chemical compositions of an object and a star's surface temperature, from which its history and future can be measured. Built at an original cost of a mere $20 million, its renovation will be upwards of $42 million. It should be fully operational sometime in 2017.

After our close look at three of the scopes, Kelly ended by informing us that the Observatory has one of the most extensive outreach programs in the world. Astronomy is an area of study that pulls just about everyone's interest into its orbit; here the hope is to increase all of our understandings of the greater complexity of the created universe than was ever imagined before, as well as to excite young people to consider careers in science and technology.

We found from what we learned and saw that our narrow vision looking at the stars with the naked eye actually opens out to a galactic panorama that continues to expand and excite all who study it through these deep eyes into the cosmos. What struck my wife and me was the perspective that a telescope can engender in the viewer; it pulled us out of our small world view to consider a vastness that allows us to see our personal and earthly conflicts through a much larger lens. We found the entire experience both humbling and liberating.

For further information:

    www.mcdonaldobservatory.org
    www.mcdonaldobservatory.org/visitors
    www.mcdonaldobservatory.org/research
    www.stardate.org
    www.stardate.org/teachers/activities

The Harlan J. Smith Telescope/ photo by the author

14

WE NEED THE DEAD IN ORDER TO LIVE FULLY

There were humans long before there was history.

~Yuval Noah Harari, *Sapiens: A Brief History of Humankind*, 3

November 2017

I step into my study at 4:00 a.m. most mornings. I am immediately surrounded by the dead in this mausoleum that houses hundreds of books and journals of those who have gone before and left their traces in words, paintings, music and sculpture. So many of *their* thoughts were derived from the dead who went before *them.* They live powerfully in their work and many of them continue to shape both culture and civilization. When we cite them or recall them, we summon the dead back into life. Photographs on my file cabinets reveal a combination of the living mingling agreeably with the now deceased.

In one of the most profound books I have read recently on the importance of the dead in our lives, conversations between archetypal psychologist James Hillman and the editor of C.G. Jung's *The Red Book*, historian Sonu Shamdasani, continue to spiral back to the crucial place occupied by the dead in life. They agree with Jung of the crucial link and necessity of contacting the dead, for they bear "the weight of human history" (*Lament* 66). Our lives cannot be complete without the presence of the dead; they live within us and around us and through us; they will not be confined to cemeteries and mausoleums or urns holding their ashes. I am, to make the point, revising this essay on Easter Sunday morning, when the dead Christ is resurrected back into our spiritual and imaginal life as a living reality. It is no accident of history that Easter is one of the most important days of worship and remembrance in the Christian calendar. Nor is the celebration of *El Dia de los Muertos*. Souls need the dead to further develop their own narratives, the roots of which span back and down into our heritage, personal and collective.

Without the dead's presence in our lives, and this Hillman and Shamdasani imply, one cannot discover fully one's own myth: "Joe Campbell would say *myth* is the hero, not the hero myth, but *myth* is the hero, *myth* is the thing that enlivens, myth is the actual psychic energy expressed in language and forms and figures. Myth is the metaphor that translates libido into configurations" (*Lament* 64). That's a lot to take in and ponder. But I don't think we can really bring the dead into the conversation without their being accompanied by the crucial importance of myth in that retrieval. The soul needs both myth and the dead, if not the *myth of the dead* in our lives.

One writer, not unlike Jung himself in his journey recounted in *The Red Book, Liber Novus,* and now himself inhabiting the creases of history, was so bold as to enter the realm of the dead to seek their wisdom, their suffering and the forces that bore down on their wayward lives, as well as their purgative journey towards redemption, and then to write a history of his experiences. In his travels through hell, purgatory and heaven he met dozens, if not hundreds of the dead. The Italian epic poet Dante Alighieri (1265-1321)—we mark the dead with their birthday and deathday—has given us one of the grandest records of the imagination of the dead as a living mortal, Dante himself, passes through their terrain guided by the shade of the dead, the classical poet, Virgil. Here the living and the dead cooperate in Dante's continued awakening. A more contemporary writer, Robert Pogue Harrison, expresses so many eloquent insights into the dead's relation to the living:

> The dead depend on the living to preserve their authority, heed their concerns, and keep them going in their afterlives. In return, they help us to know ourselves, give form to our lives, organize our social relations, and restrain our destructive impulses. (*Dominion* 158)

Our culture today has a renewed interest in tracing one's lineage to see where our deeper origins reside as well as who our full display of ancestors were. In some way we are reconfigured or even reborn through such tapping into a past, the terms of which we have not known before. The power of the dead carry within themselves the power of myth. Now to three stories of the dead.

Some years ago, my wife and I learned that the oldest hominid yet discovered intact, by the name of Lucy, was being exhibited at the Houston Museum of Natural History. She had earned the reputation of being the world's most famous fossil. Now fossils in themselves are fascinating. I understand them as dehydrated facts of life in another container; they carry the residue of history like no other species. Some deep desire in both of us collectively loomed up; we *had to* pilgrimage to Houston to gaze on her remains. Some callings cannot be reasoned through as a way to explain them.

Lucy was/is a tiny woman who lived an estimated 3.2 million years ago in an area of Ethiopia, and the magnetic draw to Houston grew partially from the fact that we would not see a replica of her but her abiding *original person.* Not even at her site in Ethiopia is her original body shown; tourists have to be satisfied with her replica.

The museum was packed and the line extensive already at mid-morning on a Sunday. Did curiosity alone bring so many to this locale to peer through the looking glass, one of the most powerful telescopes on the planet, back 3.2 million years? Well, yes, but; something deeper stirred in my wife and me and assuredly in others waiting their turn to peer into prehistory. Let me offer that Lucy takes all who see or even read about her both *back and down,* a descent into the personal and collective psyche of each of us as part of her species. She is the ancestor of all of us. For we felt, standing and gazing down at her remarkably preserved body, with fingernails and a bit of hair still intact, skin curled but visible, solid teeth that could still chew through roots and plants-- a strong sense of relatedness.

She also conjured up in us a sense of our own personal past as well as our own inevitable future. The dead are indispensable aids for our imaginations in seeing ourselves in life. Without the dead, the living would lose a part of themselves which could include something dead in us requiring new life. So, the dead may be understood as an indispensable partner of our living myths. The dead have the capacity to awaken something deceased in us, something perhaps asking for renewal, remembrance and reintegration. What it tapped in my wife and me is the deep lineage that we are part of, not just as humanoids, but as forms of life that are part of the universe's record who exists and existed within it. We looked with fascination and awe at her teeth still embedded in her ancient jawbone. We looked at her fingers that curved and had the capacity to hold and to carry things because she walked upright and so had the freedom to carry items, including her own children.

Lucy's presence in her original state stimulated our historical imagination to wonder, to ponder who we are and what we are as a species and even to meditate on our own destiny, as Lucy may have thought of her own. We wondered what might have been her thoughts and feelings as she walked in search of certain plants to prepare or to eat on the spot? What gave her joy? What caused her suffering? Who did she like and not like in the group she may have lived within? What dangers did she face that required constant vigilance and perhaps protection from others? What children did she perhaps lose at birth, or to sickness or death by other humanoids or beasts? All we could do is wonder at her story.

Seeking after origins, the beginnings and then the continuity of ourselves and things, is one of the most mythic impulses imbedded in the consciousness of our communal longings. We yearn for our past, both as remembered and as imagined. We also yearn for knowledge of the future, where we are headed personally and collectively. Uncertainty can make us very nervous and ungrounded. The dead are marvelous presences who help us remain grounded, rooted to the present because their own roots reach back in time whose years we cannot fathom.

For that instinct alone, to know something of our origins, it was worth the pilgrimage to Lucy's shrine to peer for a few moments through the glass of prehistory, or perhaps better to say, through a glass and a mirror of history to a more primal and animated past and at a sweet leathery face looking up at us that held in its visage the entire race of humanity. No text could have benefited us more with such a tender power as did she. We felt the presence of our collective mother in Lucy's animated, still body.

The word *human* derives from the Latin *humanitas* and *humando*, meaning "to bury." We humans bury not just to separate from the dead but to humanize the ground in which we build our worlds and found our histories, according to Harrison. Humanity means in part a way of being mortal and relating to the dead. To be human means above all to bury, to bury in the humus of the earth. Human and humans stem from the same root word (*Dominion* xi). Human, humus, humility are all related. The word *nature* is from nasci=to be born. As human beings we are born from the dead; they bear us up. Such are the two sides of our "human nature." To be human is to translate our mortality into history, for we are, finally, temporal beings. The dead help us keep this singular reality in mind.

A second story: When I was on a three-and-a-half-month pilgrimage to monasteries and Zen Buddhist centers in five western states in 1998, I found myself one afternoon at my second monastery, early in my voyage, sitting by a fish pond at a Carmelite Retreat House in Napa Valley, California. The monastic dog, Dusty, was always by my side because in part, I was the only retreatant in residence so his choices were seriously scant. I won out. While sitting there watching the bullfrogs rise from below the surface, I suddenly felt the presence of my father sitting beside me on the bench. I must tell you that he had joined the population of the dead two years earlier.

He wanted to tell me about his life as the father of five of us as well as his alcoholism that kept him from doing many of the things we thought regular fathers did with their kids. Our friends had such fathers, so why did we draw the short straw? Now I have to say that his presence was so palpable, that when we finished our conversation which would become one of many subsequently, I walked back to my hermitage where my Ford Ranger was parked, cleared out the passenger seat of CDs, a few books and a jacket as well as a small cooler, and put them all in the back so he could have his own space to ride with me, that is, if he planned to accompany me farther. He stayed with me for the entire three months remaining, not speaking often, but when he did what he had to share with me in many instances, reflected what I had inherited from him. Here is a passage from *A Pilgrimage Beyond Belief,* the spiritual memoir I wrote from the notes I had compiled each day as well as other remembrances:

> When I finished reading a passage from the Benedictine monk, Thomas Merton, I thought of my father's voice, his actions, his tormented life as an alcoholic, a disease that had a thick core and a very unsettling vein running

throughout my family of Irish Catholics. He visited me powerfully now as he would do in many succeeding monasteries. Perhaps he now wanted to be heard, or even noticed, by me, in the silence of an autumn evening, when leaves themselves were falling to the earth, occupied with their own dying. Perhaps in this silence, the voice of my father, who was so reticent in his sober life, now wanted a conversation; I hoped that I could garner the forgiveness in me to oblige his insistent yearning (98).

Later I was to read in Thomas W. Laqueur's masterful work, *The Work of the Dead: A Cultural History of Mortal Remains,* the following helpful insight: "The history of the work of the dead is a history of how they dwell in us—individually and communally. It is a history of how we imagine them to be, how they give meaning to our lives, how they structure public spaces, politics and time" (17). I find this insight very appropriate as I enter my third and last story relating the living to the dead.

This final story is first one about the living. It relates the story of a woman in Atlanta who taught me something about the dead when I gave a talk there on the book and read some of the passages from *Pilgrimage Beyond Belief,* wherein my father was present. When I had finished and entertained several participants' questions and observations, she approached me as I was gathering my material; after a moment of hesitation she asked: did you REALLY see your father? Was he REALLY present to you so you could have a conversation with him? I did not want to turn into Bill Clinton at this juncture, nonetheless I had to ask her what she meant by REALLY. I went on to describe to her that my father was a presence in my travels for the better part of three months, and that we conversed often.

At that moment she began to weep. I asked her if I had said something to offend her. "No," she answered, "but I have not spoken to my own mother, who is still alive, for 15 years. Listening to you, I am beginning to feel some hope that after she dies the two of us may be able to have some real conversations that are missing in our lives right now." And with that she turned and left. I end by saying to you all that her remark and her hope was sufficient for me to have spent the time and energy in writing and then revising the story of my journey with God and my father.

Question: If you could have a conversation with any of the dead, not just family members or friends, but of course include them, who would you choose? What would be the draw for you to that person or pet? And, what, if anything, might you hope to learn from them and perhaps, about you?

Works Cited

Harari, Noah Yuval. *Sapiens: A Brief History of Humankind*. Harper Perennial, 2015.

Harrison, Robert Pogue. *The Dominion of the Dead*. U of Chicago P, 2003.

Hillman, James and Sonu Shamdasani. *Lament of the Dead: Psychology After Jung's* Red Book. W.W. Norton, 2013.

Laqueur, Thomas W. *The Work of the Dead: A Cultural History of Mortal Remains*. Princeton UP, 2015.

Selzer, Richard. *Raising the Dead: A Doctor's Encounter with His Own Mortality*. Viking Penguin, 1993.

Slattery, Dennis Patrick. *A Pilgrimage Beyond Belief: Spiritual Journeys Through Christian and Buddhist Monasteries of the American West*. Preface by Peter C. Phan. Foreword by Thomas Moore. Angelico Press, 2017. Originally published in 2004 by Jossey-Bass as *Grace in the Desert: Awakening to the Gifts of Monastic Life*.

15

LIBERAL LEARNING AND ITS BENEVOLENT CONSEQUENCES[*]

More than one voice has called our current level of cultural discourse a crisis of civility. Acrimony, being right, crushing the opposition, spreading alternative realities to fit individual agendas, have all put the nation on a collective and narrow bandwidth of conversation as well as caused moral wounding in the collective consciousness, whatever one's political stands.

We, the authors, have spent approximately 90 years in the classroom and have taught students from grades one through Ph.D. candidates. We believe that what has been lost sight of in current discussions that go beyond the posturings of position politics is the value of liberal learning; we choose that term over the more passive term "education," which is generally understood as something one "gets" rather than a manner of engaging both the material and one another in the imaginative process of learning. Rather than content, we believe that the values inherent in liberal learning, which includes disciplines like literature, sociology, philosophy, myth, rhetoric, politics, religion and history, go well beyond the content of these areas of study.

---

[*] Originally published as "Liberal Learning Can Lead to Fruitful Discourse." Co-authored with Dr. Roger Barnes. *San Antonio Express-News*, September 4th, 2018, 17-A.

More than the content of various ways of knowing are the attitudes and perspectives that liberal learning fosters, which in our minds includes, but is far from limited to, the following descriptions:

- An emphasis on imagination as a way of knowing that, in conjunction with reasoned inquiry, allows for a fuller sensibility to be cultivated in one's pursuit not only of knowledge but finally, of wisdom.

- A way into self-discovery and an avenue for deepening self-awareness and a more comprehensive consciousness than ideological pursuits and defenses allow for.

- The above also implicates the way that liberal learning can aid each student in forming their more coherent narrative, that is, the myth they are living and is living them, in order to become a more whole and compassionate human being.

- Recognizing one's place individually and nationally in a historical continuum that reflects who we are as historical, social, psychological, spiritual and uniquely individual agents existing within a shared mythos. Such an ambition would include reconnecting with the older wisdom traditions that have guided our ancestors for millennia. From them we can draw helpful and fruitful analogies between past cultures and our current expanding ones.

- Recognizing and cultivating how each discipline in liberal learning promotes its own form of imagining, contemplating, meditating and remembering, all as valid ways of knowing that, together, offer a far richer and fertile ground for understanding our place in a collective continuum of humanity's strivings for the improvement of all classes, ethnicities and races. Such a perspective frees us from the often-crushing demands and limits of tribalism whose diet of understanding extends no further than its own hard-baked fantasies.

- One of the most crucial end results of liberal learning is not only the restoration and cultivation of authentic and respectful dialogue, especially between opposing points of views and belief systems, but also the cultivation of compassion, empathy and respect for ourselves and others through a deeper sense of self, with its ideals and its shadows, a vision of our common heritage in the context of a shared common good. Such a move demands that fear no longer be the motivating or leading emotion in facing the difference in and of others.

- Liberal learning, then, fosters courage as a co-equal partner with compassion.

- Finally, the value of liberal learning in the context of the above processes and attitudes is to restore and further a truly democratic people and its purposes that is unafraid of facing head-on what differentiates us, while at the same time promoting what we share in the core of our humanness. The paradox inherent in such a perspective is that our individual differences may be the bedrock for our authentic unity and accord. Both yearn to be celebrated in liberal learning.

- Rather than "follow the money," liberal learning encourages each active member of the community to "follow one's meaning,"; only with a conscious awareness of a broader and more inclusive vision of one's life can we find again and further the democratic ideals that make us the unique nation we are; we gain strength and self-awareness as a people when we are in on-going conversations with the nations of the world as well as with individuals we live next door to.

For Further Reading

Cowan, Donald and Louise Cowan, editors. *Classic Texts and the Nature of Authority: An Account of a Principals' Institute Conducted by the Dallas Institute of Humanities and Culture.* Dallas Institute Publications, 1993.

Slattery, Dennis Patrick and Jennifer Leigh Selig, editors. *Reimagining Education: Essays on Reviving the Soul of Learning.* Mandorla Books, 2019.

Slattery, Dennis Patrick, Jennifer Leigh Selig, et al., editors. *Re-Ensouling Education: Essays on the Importance of the Humanities in Schooling the Soul.* Mandorla Books, 2019.

16

THE TRUTH IS HARD: HISTORY MAY REPEAL ITSELF*

Recently my wife and I returned from a five-day holiday in New York City. High on our list for this first of what we hope are many visits, were tours by boat to the Statue of Liberty, a magnificent gift to the United States in the harbor that we had seen only in photos. Then on to Ellis Island to walk through the rooms that so many immigrants, primarily from Eastern and Western Europe arriving there by ship, were taken to be registered, examined both physically and psychologically and then either granted entry or turned away. We learned that only about 2% of all those who were processed in a month were rejected, but that number often totaled over a thousand individuals. We wanted to see these two American icons that greeted 12 million people from 1892-1920s seeking a new life in this land of promise.

With many other tourists, we walked through one room after another. Some were for physical examinations, others for language proficiency and still others were for psychological assessments. We could feel the presence of decades of flows of citizens seeking a new myth, a new way of living, and new opportunities for their creative growth. We also felt the presence of so many family members that also

---

*Originally published as "Truthfulness has Healing Powers."'" Opinion" page of New Braunfels' *The Herald-Zeitung*, Sunday, April 1st, 2018. 5-A.

sensed promise and a chance for something better as they came within site of the magnificent statue holding her torch high, as if to light the way for the optimism that sailed into New York's busy harbor. From there we boated back and took the subway to the center of Manhattan.

We were surprised by an unplanned third site that came into our view: the front window of the Sachs Fifth Avenue store across a side street from St. Patrick's Cathedral. On its window in white lettering were the following series of observations on a fragile and endangered species today that we thought deserved as much attention as the two welcoming emblems we had just visited. Together, Liberty, Immigration and The Truth have over the decades shared a rich and compatible heritage that today is being renegotiated, if not challenged, anew. Here is what greeted us from behind the glass window, which we photographed to ponder later:

The truth is hard.
The truth is hidden.
The truth must be pursued.
The truth is hard to hear.
The truth is rarely simple.
The truth is rarely obvious.
The truth doesn't take sides.
The truth is not red or blue.
The truth is necessary.
The truth can't be glossed over.
The truth has no agenda.
The truth is hard to accept.
The truth pulls no punches.
The truth is worth defending.
The truth requires taking a stand.
The truth is more important now than ever.

The New York Times

We left our first pilgrimage to New York City with images of the statue, the interior of Ellis Island's screening facilities, the friendly and helpful New Yorkers who lived there, and a photo of the above set of truths. All of these images and words seemed in our minds of equal value and worthy of reflection.

For the reader to contemplate:

- Is there a line from the above list that stands out for you or has particular relevance for you?
- What state or condition is "The Truth" in today's world?
- In your mind, is "The Truth" worth protecting or does it mean less today than in previous times?
- What might be the deep connection between "The Truth" and the health or illness of our democracy?
- Is there, to your mind, a "Cult of Untruth" gaining in status and strength in our culture today?
- *The Declaration of Independence* has as its beginning credo: "We hold these truths to be self-evident. . . ." I found it so valuable to return to this document and reread these Truths from the Founders.

Further Reading

Gladstone, Brooke. *The Trouble with Reality: A Rumination on Moral Panic in Our Time.* Workman Publishing, 2017.

Harris, Sam. *Lying.* Edited by Annaka Harris. Four Elephants Press, 2013.

Jacoby, Susan. *The Age of American Unreason in a Culture of Lies.* Vintage, 2018.

Lakoff, George. *Don't Think of an Elephant! Know Your Values and Frame the Debate.* Chelsea Green Publishing, 2004.

Orwell, George. *Orwell on Truth.* Houghton Mifflin Harcourt, 2019.

Snyder, Timothy. *On Tyranny: Twenty Lessons from the Twentieth Century.* Tim Duggan Books, 2017.

17

THE SCAPEGOAT SOLUTION[*]

We must think of the monstrous as beginning with the lack of differentiation, with a process that, though it has no effect on reality, does affect the perception of it.

~René Girard, *The Scapegoat*, 33

It seems to be a natural human tendency to scapegoat others—their ideas, appearance, beliefs, their otherness—in order to make one feel less threatened by differences and to shore up a weak and impotent self-image. History is riddled with individuals, entire peoples and their beliefs, who became victims of those in power, to be blamed and scourged because of the fear they roil up in others. René Girard, cited at the top of this essay, also observes that "the whole range of victims can be found in myths, . . ." (32). It is an ancient psychic and political strategy. Certainly, the border-crossing migrants at our southern borders are one of the most recent stigmatized body of people to fall under the axe of scapegoat. Like so many collectives of victims, they are often the most lacking in power, wealth or influence and so are easy to malign, stereotype and exile.

Scapegoating as a strategy and most recently far-too-often a solution, is easy to execute because no proof is required, only feelings of malice toward an Other repeated with a furious frequency to

---

[*] Originally published as "Employing the Easy Scapegoat Solution." Opinion page of New Braunfels' *The Herald-Zeitung,* Sunday, July 7th, 2019, p. 4A.

convince the unreflective of its validity. Here is how this dismissive strategy works:

- Make the scapegoat a dangerous, reckless and threatening Other.
- Choose those who have little or no power or voice so there will be a minimum of retaliation.
- Choose those who are most vulnerable and disposable.
- Select those who are easy to keep in place—unless of course their numbers become overwhelming and they find their collective political or social voice of authority to strike back.
- Keep the facts about the scapegoat at bay, hidden or, if they leak out, distort, fictionalize and package them in the wrappings of outrage.
- Use language to shape them as criminal, untrustworthy, threatening and infectious.
- Smother those scapegoated with innuendoes, untruths, half-truths, deceitful motives and sinister intentions.
- Repeat the message ten thousand times, as is done often in Aldous Huxley's *Brave New World*. Over time it will assume the appearance of "truth."

A recent film my wife and I watched is titled *Swimming in Auschwitz*, a documentary on Netflix in which six women from the Holocaust relate their stories of survival. In one of the film clips was the slogan: "If you are a Jew you are a Criminal."

The question we must ask as this new scapegoat assumes greater prominence is: What does the scapegoat serve in its creators or those who willingly and unquestioningly serve it? Well, several venues.

- The scapegoat protects those creating it from having to face their own shadows—their inferiority, their lust for power, their own vulnerabilities, their own fragility, their own inadequate knowledge base and their own haunting demons.
- The scapegoat protects their creator from any open dialogue or conversation about their true nature and

needs. Scapegoating does not hold up in authentic conversations.

- Scapegoating forecloses on dialogue, understanding or compassion for the Other who, if seen as they are, reflect aspects of our own flawed human nature.
- Scapegoating protects one from any disruption of the familiar, the comfortable, from standard beliefs, prejudices, ideas and from the reality that the world is in continual flux and change.
- Scapegoating protects their creators from becoming conscious on any level and allows them to continue to float in the warm current of their own entangled complexes—personal, ideological, and national.
- Scapegoating protects its creators from their own woundedness, their own afflictions, limitations and shortcomings—it further establishes the fantasy of oneself that one must protect at all costs.
- Scapegoating keeps the ancient relation of Master/Slave fantasy alive and intact.
- Scapegoating also promotes and cultivates its own corrosive effects on the human spirit of both parties. It not only feeds on itself but also self-procreates. The distortion of the scapegoat can then migrate into a greater monster than it was at its inception.
- Scapegoating allows its creator to cement one's basest impulses into the minds of others while it brutalizes rather than blesses the other as so *like* me; instead it emphasizes the difference *from* me.
- Scapegoating relies mightily on the absolute acceptance of slogans while it struggles to occlude any facts, stories or exceptions that contradict its elaborate and demonizing fictions.

Brooke Gladstone's 2017 *The Trouble with Reality: A Rumination on Moral Panic in Our Time,* refers early on in her study of false news and creating stereotypes by citing a classic work by the legendary newspaper man, Walter Lippmann. In *Public Opinion* Lippman suggested, in Gladstone's words, that it seems to be a human habit or proclivity to "pick up a salient detail about a person or group—black, white; international banker, kindergarten teacher . . . and then blithely fill in the rest of the blanks. Now we think we know them" (8). The path from stereotyping an individual or a group to scapegoating them, can be only a matter of a few yards.

So what happens when we are dished up a trait or two of a group or individual: murderers and rapists, filthy, illegal, scum, less-than-human— is that the work is done for us. Then we think, taking a slithery short-cut: "All people of this race, ethnicity, belief, poverty level are in fact X." The stereotype has been born with a gusto that gives it a life-sustaining element because now it can feed itself and feed *on* itself for further validation. Stereotypes are scapegoats *in utero* or immediately following birth. To repeat the stereotypes' qualities a thousand times begins to make it true; how could it be otherwise when I am hearing these traits everywhere? Now another monster has been manufactured, like Victor Frankenstein's lab experiment, and takes on its own life. That is another insight about stereotypes morphing with the complicit assistance from agenda-ridden others, into a scapegoat; now we have someone or something to blame, to project our own shadowy selves onto and so escape scrutiny of our own actions. Clever, no?

Gladstone affirms that there is another powerful element to exploit in stereotypes: they "create the patterns that compose our world. It is not necessarily the world we would like it to be, he [Lippman] says, it is simply the kind of world we expect it to be" (9).

Works Cited

Girard, René. *The Scapegoat.* Translated by Yvonne Freccero. John Hopkins UP, 1986.
Gladstone, Brooke. *The Trouble with Reality: A Rumination on Moral Panic in Our Time.* Workman Publishing, 2017.

Further Reading

Deardorff, Daniel. *The Other Within: The Genius of Deformity in Myth, Culture and Psyche.* Heaven and Earth Publishing, 2009.

Lakoff, George. *Don't Think of an Elephant: Know Your Values and Frame Your Debate*. Chelsea Green Publishing, 2004.

Lehrer, Jonah. *How We Decide*. Houghton Mifflin Harcourt, 2009.

Lippmann, Walter J. *Public Opinion: How People Decide; The Role of News, Propaganda and Manufactured Consent in Modern Democracy and Political Elections*. Adansonia P, 2018.

Morrison, Toni. *The Origin of Others*. Harvard UP, 2017.

Newberg, Andrew, M.D. *Why We Believe What We Believe: Uncovering Our Biological Need for Meaning, Spirituality, and Truth*. Free Press, 2006.

Ricoeur, Paul. *Oneself as Another*. Translated by Kathleen Blamey. U of Chicago P, 1992.

Romanyshyn, Robert. *Victor Frankenstein, the Monster and the Shadows of Technology: The Frankenstein Prophecies*. Routledge, 2019.

18

JUST WHAT IS MYTHING IN YOUR LIFE?[*]

It is unfortunate that in our current world the word "myth" is still maligned as something related to a lie, or to what is untrue, and is opposed to "fact." Myth is something to be done away with because it is counter to what is true, some mistakenly assume. The irony here is that such a definition of myth grew out of a period in history when fact, measurement and quantification were seen as the only means of measuring, quantifying and predicting reality. The Enlightenment extolled reason and scientific veracity with one hand as it relegated myth to the dust bin of history and fable with the other. That in itself is a myth, namely a belief system, a way of seeing and understanding that sidelined myth as a valid and viable way of knowing.

Currently myth has weak standing in our nation's educational curriculum. Generally speaking, there is not one Introduction to Mythology course in 12 years of public and often, in private schools as well. Never mind that many of the science fiction films that young and old flock to are, in many cases, based on ancient mythic stories. Why the disconnect? Why not view a section of a Star Wars film, for instance, in the classroom as a way to open a discussion on the reality of myths?

Before the rise of reason, of quantifying and eventually controlling the world's matter, as well as prior to philosophy as a system of

---

* Originally published as "Just What is Mything in Your Life?" Opinion page of New Braunfels' *The Herald-Zeitung*, March 10th, 2019. A-4 to A-5.

understanding, myths were the preferred way to knowledge. Simply put, the word *myth* means story, narrative, plot and for untold millennia humans told one another stories to impart what had happened to them, what they had learned, or how to survive; even their desires and hopes for the future were wrapped in the container of narratives. Just as importantly, the prevailing language of myth is metaphor, symbol, figures of speech and images. I like how David Feinstein puts it: "A myth is a loom on which we weave the raw materials of daily experience into a coherent story" (*The Mythic Path* 20). We can all grasp with a little reflection the power of this metaphor. All of us weave the events of our lives into fabrics of fables and narratives that shape and contain our identity as a person; the weave also reveals the patterns that give our lives purpose. Such a process is no less true for entire cultures and civilizations.

The key word above is "coherence." A myth, be it personal or collective, brings the disparate parts of our lives together into a meaningful whole. Without such a coherent meaning, a form of psychic mucilage to hold our lives together, our lives are full of holes. And with coherence another element is included: meaning. A life without meaning is a life without a coherent myth. Some have called myths belief systems. True enough, but like anything organic, our belief systems need periodic reviews and assessments to see if those beliefs formed years or decades ago, still hold up as viable ways for us to organize and cohere our lives. Myths have shelf lives as well as any other perishable and need to be discarded when they no longer serve our life's pilgrimage. Myths guide us in understanding not just *who* we are but *why* we are.

To access one's myth, one can ask: what am I called to in this life? What is my destiny, my purpose and my path? To answer such questions is to invite one's myth into the conversation. Most people do not know the myth they are living, or have only fleeting glimpses, especially in times of disruption. Illness, surgery, loss of a relationship, family, a job, a purpose for living—all of these can force one to pause and ask: "what am I doing in this life? What is no longer working for me and where do I need to change?" Again, these are mythic questions. Not only individuals but nations can find themselves at an impasse where they reach a critical point in what they believe and begin to reflect on their basic values. Values are one of many ways that a myth reveals its presence. Listen to someone you have known or someone you have just met. In the story they choose to tell you are values and a sense of their identity imbedded within the folds of the narratives you hear. The famous writer who gave us narratives of his time as a concentration camp survivor, Elie Wiesel, commented that "God made man because he loves stories" (qtd. in *The Stories We Live By* 17).

The most popular mythologist of the last century was Joseph Campbell (1904-87). As a comparative mythologist, he spent his life comparing world mythologies and perceived the common patterns in narratives that so many of them shared. He was also one of the few to grasp the power of the media to disseminate not just information but knowledge. His 6-part series on PBS, *The Power of Myth,* in conversation with Bill Moyers, is still the most viewed program on public television. His book of the same name is a bedrock text for grasping the ways that we are both living *in* a myth and being lived *by* a myth. He says early on in his conversations with Bill Moyers that "Myth helps you to put your mind in touch with this experience of being alive. It tells you what the experience is" (*The Power of Myth* 6). I would add that myths assist in your challenge to become more conscious of who you are and what relationship you have with the rest of the world.

All myths, Campbell believes, are metaphors for actions and events in both our interior life and the external world we move in each day; both can aid us in becoming more aware of life's meaning. "Follow Your Bliss" reached bumper sticker status many years ago. By this he meant: follow the path that arises within you, that serves a constructive purpose, rather than following a path dictated to you. If you follow a prescribed road, one already showing traces of others who have trod it before you, then you are living another's myth, not yours. But he was no sentimentalist; he believed following one's bliss created its own unique assortment of blisters. Myths help us suffer into an awareness of ourselves. World mythologies reveal that no one can avoid suffering in some measure.

Some of the current myths that govern our country include: the myth of growth, the myth of economics, the myth of technology, the myth of consumption, the myth of safety, the myth of self-protection as well as some, perhaps diminishing forms of the myths of equality, freedom and opportunity. Our myths reveal themselves most pointedly and poignantly in the political and advertising worlds. Of course, what shows find their way into our television sets and movie theaters are also good barometers of our values. In addition, look at any country and note what holidays they celebrate together and you get a pulse read on what myths carry their values, what they believe in, even if only partially. A wonderful short story by the American writer Shirley Jackson entitled "The Lottery" reveals what happens when belief in a myth has been lost, disavowed or forgotten, but the rituals that once organically supported it continue to be practiced mechanically and senselessly and can invite violence. Violence is often the consequence of a myth that has frozen into a cadaver of an ideology. Her entire story can be read online.

When a myth that has heretofore united a people begins to unravel into tribal myths that divide rather than maintain an essential unity, that myth is stressed and strained, perhaps into distorted forms of itself. When a myth is called into question it may need to be revised and/or reasserted with exceptional vigor. Such a crisis can be a signal that parts of a myth need to be rethought, let go of, or revitalized.

Being reflective rather than reactionary about this condition can be constructive and replenishing not only for us as individuals, but for entire nations. Being mythically aware is an essential element of being fully human. Listen closely, then, to people's stories; you are listening to their myth delivered in a unique narrative container. Follow the particulars of their stories; you will discern some of the patterns that give their life purpose.

Works Cited

Campbell, Joseph. *The Power of Myth*. Doubleday, 1988.

Feinstein, David and Stanley Krippner. *The Mythic Path: Discovering the Guiding Stories of Your Past—Creating a Vision for Your Future*. Putnam Books, 1997.

McAdams, Dan. P. *The Stories We Live By: Personal Myths and the Making of the Self*. Guilford Press, 1998.

Further Reading

Bond, D. Stephenson. *Living Myth: Personal Meaning as a Way of Life*. Shambhala Publications, 1993.

Campbell, Joseph. *The Hero with a Thousand Faces*. New World Library, 2008.

McAdams, Dan. P. *Power, Intimacy and the Life Story: Personological Inquiries into Identity*. Guilford Press, 1988.

---. *The Redemptive Self: Stories Americans Live By*. Oxford UP, 2006.

Slattery, Dennis Patrick. *Riting Myth, Mythic Writing: Plotting Your Personal Story*. Fisher King Press, 2012.

---. *From War to Wonder: Recovering Your Personal Myth Through Homer's Odyssey*. Mandorla Books, 2019.

Taylor, Daniel. *The Healing Power of Stories: Creating Yourself Through the Stories of Your Life*. Doubleday, 1996.

19

THE YEARNING TO CREATE:
A UNIVERSAL IMPULSE[*]

We believe that deep creativity can be cultivated. It's a way of being in the world, a way of seeing the world, and an enchanted way at that.

~Deborah Anne Quibell, *Deep Creativity: Seven Ways to Spark Your Creative Spirit*, 5

I like to write and, perhaps more importantly, I have a consistent desire to express myself through the written word. I was somehow led into a profession where two loves of mine, reading and writing, comprised a large part of this life project.

I have over the years written several volumes of poetry, one co-authored novel with a close friend, and an assortment of books of essays on a variety of topics that interested me then and now. I have also written a spiritual memoir recounting a 14-week pilgrimage through monasteries, retreat centers and Zen Buddhist enclaves in five western states. I have taken both pottery and painting classes from teachers at the top of their respective fields. While you may or may not have engaged any of the above, my guess is that you have found other outlets for this deep hunger in all of us to create, to make something, to feel the frustrations and satisfactions of pushing yourself into new

---

[*] Originally published as "The Yearning to Create: A Universal Impulse." Opinion page of New Braunfels' *The Herald-Zeitung*, Sunday May 26, 2019. A-4-5.

areas of crafting something new, from a piece of music to a life well-lived.

This deep desire in each of us to shape, create and construct is a universal yearning that we may respond to at various moments in our lives or simply pass on its persistence. Either way, the yearning is or has knocked on your door in one form or another, and not once but many times. So insistent was this drive not only to create but to think creatively *about* creativity that three of us began writing on this topic about four years ago. The current result is a book on creativity. We titled it *Deep Creativity: Seven Ways to Spark Your Creative Spirit* (2019), which I am happy to inform you was recently awarded first place in the category "Creativity & Innovation" by the Nautilus Book Awards committee in a national competition.

I bring this product of our creativity up, of course, to let you know it exists, but more importantly, to share a few ideas that we discovered about this rich and mysterious element of being human. We were surprised to discover how far-reaching the act of creation extends deeply into some of the hidden corners of our lives and how it can cultivate a richer, more meaningful form of being most fully ourselves. The act of creating fosters a new iteration of the world's emanation; the world is remade in part, when we enter fully this mysterious urging gnawing in the soul. In the process, our own self of ourselves also undergoes some new iteration of consciousness that may be as spiritual as it is psychological.

One of the most interesting recognitions we discovered is that, at its most basic level, creativity is an attitude. Not aptitude. Not a skill set. Not training. Creativity as attitude is a perspective on life and ourselves in creative relationship to it, as Deborah's quote underneath the title of this essay attests to. From this basic insight, we discovered many others, only a few of which I have space to accommodate. Here are some of the most crucial ones as we discovered in the journey of shaping our book. I have changed the wording in some instances but kept the intention of these principles, all fifteen of which are in the book. You are encouraged to add to these by means of your own creative projects and achievements:

- **Deep Creativity is receptive:** Here we open ourselves up to the world, to what appears, to what pulls our attention towards it; we make ourselves available for inspiration. Inspiration has its origin in "to be inspired," or "to be inspirited." Our receptivity is measured in large part by our ability to be porous, open and curious about the world.

- **Deep Creativity is spiritual:** I have added this dimension; it calls to our spiritual nature, not necessarily through the aperture of any systematic religious belief, though it could. Here, however we found that spiritual relates to that most mysterious part of our being, one that cannot be explained but it can certainly be experienced deeply. It is also transcendent because it has the capacity to lift us out of ourselves.

- **Deep Creativity is idiosyncratic:** No two of us will be drawn to the same thing or in the same way, and our creation of it will be as unique and novel as our fingerprint. When we create, we reveal some of the most unique features of who and what we are. "Tell me what you yearn to create and I will tell you who you are" has some validity here.

- **Deep Creativity is healing:** Our creative acts, in whatever form they assume, may be the source of our self-healing and when shared with others, whether it be product or service, may assuredly be healing for them as well.

- **Deep Creativity is participatory:** When we allow ourselves to move into creative space on whatever level we choose, we join a population of creatives who engage their lives in similar ways. In the painting classes I attend once a week, now for eight years, I am enthused and inspired by those I paint with. I am nourished in my own work by their processes and products. Our community is held together by how diverse we are in what we choose to paint or draw; we all participate in one another's efforts, be they ones that fall short or exceed our individual expectations.

- **Deep Creativity is reciprocal**: In the act of creating we are both subject and object of our efforts and achievements. As we create, we are created. What I make in the world I make simultaneously in myself and perhaps in others. Creating is its own form of dialogue with the world and within ourselves. I talk to myself through everything I create.

- **Deep Creativity is embodied**: When we come to creativity, we come *with* our senses, we come *to* our senses. We are fully sensate and conscious of the mystery of the world through all our senses. Creative yearning stimulates the senses to be more sensitive to life's presence. In creating the body is not left behind but more fully enfleshed in what we shape.

All of these qualities of creativity lead us to a hunger to risk something, to be courageous in the face of newness that, quite frankly, and I am a good illustration of this point, we may fail at or fall short of achieving what we had planned to accomplish. But creativity is aspirational as well as inspirational; falling short and noticing why is to take another step towards self-understanding. Falling short is no reason to cease breaking new ground in our lives, regardless of our age. The urge to create is timeless and ageless, which makes it possible to put our feet into this mysterious miracle that we call life and to leave a trace for having lived it. I end by suggesting that creativity is forgiving; it honors the reality that one dared to step forward to risk something important: their own limitations.

Work Cited

Quibell, Deborah Anne, Jennifer Leigh Selig and Dennis Patrick Slattery. *Deep Creativity: Seven Ways to Spark Your Creative Spirit.* Shambhala Publications, 2019.

Further Reading

Bohm, David. *On Creativity*. Routledge, 2004.

Fassler, Joe. *Light the Dark: Writers on Creativity, Inspiration and the Artistic Process*. Penguin, 2017.

Isaacson, Walter. *Leonardo Da Vinci*. Simon and Schuster, 2017.

Savage, Roz. *Stop Drifting, Start Rowing: One Woman's Search for Happiness and Meaning Alone on the Atlantic*. Hay House, 2013.

Spitz, Ellen Handler. *Art and Psyche: A Study in Psychoanalysis and Aesthetics*. Yale UP, 1985.

20

REMEMBERING TONI MORRISON[*]

One of America's finest writers of both fiction and nonfiction died on August 6th of this year, 2019, at the age of 88. Toni Morrison was born in 1931 and raised in Lorain, Ohio as Chloe Wofford. She took her husband's last name when she married, then changed her name to Toni, largely because people struggled to pronounce Chloe correctly.

While a prolific fiction writer of such works as *The Bluest Eye, Beloved, Jazz, Paradise, A Mercy, Home* and *God Save the Child,* among others, her best known work, *Beloved,* won the Pulitzer Prize in 1987 and the Nobel Prize in 1992, a feat rarely achieved by any writer for the same creative work.

Two other books of non-fiction, *Playing in the Dark: Whiteness and the Literary Imagination,* and in the last two years, *The Origin of Others,* were both originally offered as a series of lectures she delivered at Harvard University in 1990 and 2016 respectively. I have taught her most popular novel, *Beloved* for many years to a large range of ages and ethnicities of students and continue to uncover fresh insights in rereading and reteaching it.

Morrison's range and depth of interest in subjects is vast: on writing and reading, the place and power of the imagination, race, class, globalization, cultural constructions of identity, memory, politics,

---

[*] Originally published as "Looking at Toni Morrison: The Passing of Wisdom." Opinion page of New Braunfels' *The Herald-Zeitung,* August 20th, 2019, p. 4.

prejudice, whiteness, literary knowledge and most pronounced, slavery, to name a small handful.

In *Playing in the Dark,* for instance, she observes that "cultural identities are formed and informed by a nation's literature, and that what seemed to be on the 'mind' of the literature of the United States was the self-conscious but highly problematic construction of the American as a new white man" (39). It could only create such a figure by contrasting it or playing it off against the black race, she suggests later. And then to this seminal question in the lectures: "In what ways does the imaginative encounter with Africanism enable white writers to think about themselves?" (*Playing* 51). Self-definition then becomes self-opposition with the Other; we define ourselves by contrast, opposition, us/them, dualism and dichotomy. Such is one potent way in which myths are formed.

The more recently published *The Origin of Others* provides a provocative sustained reflection on how we each can easily gravitate to creating "Otherness." It too has an intricate and involved history. Today, perhaps in more pronounced ways, the creation of "Otherness" has often two intentions, as Morrison describes it: as a way for an individual or group or even a nation, to gain a stronger toe-hold on what they believe by creating an Other. Her intention throughout her work, which is central to the power of this last series of lectures, is the following: "But I am determined to de-fang cheap racism, annihilate and discredit the routine, easy, available color fetish, which is reminiscent of slavery itself" (*Origin* 53). By doing so she hopes to raise to a respectable human project the rare occupation of self-reflection.

Her fundamental question in this latter collection is simple and basic: "How does one become a racist, or a sexist" since "no one is born a racist" or sexist? Her answer is that "one learns Othering not by lecture or instruction but by example." This is a deep urge in all of us for "a social/psychological need for a 'stranger,' an Other, in order to define the estranged self (the crowd seeker is always the lonely one)" (*Origin* 6).

Her research into this phenomenal need to create an "Other" was apprehended quickly by immigrants to the US; "if they wanted to become 'real' Americans they must sever or at least severely mute their ties to their native country in order to embrace their whiteness" (*Origin*

17). Color still lingers for many as the standard definition of being an American.

Late in her reflections on crafting an alien Other, Morrison suggests three constants at play in many individuals' perceptions of foreignness: 1) Menace; 2) Depravity; 3) Incomprehensibility (*Origin* 106-07). It is not difficult to see that a common driving impulse in all three of these perceptions/projections rests on fear of a threat. In such a vulnerable condition and breathing such a toxic atmosphere, one may be easily encouraged/persuaded to create and attack the "Other" through one or all of the crafted ways of perceiving someone who, by their very diversity, becomes a threatening foreign force. What does this say about an individual, a group or a nation that so fiercely fears the unfamiliar? It feels to me, reading and rereading this last series of insightful talks, that fear deadens the soul and that one misdirected response to recovering that deadened part of oneself is to become violent towards what one has never had a conversation with within themselves.

Morrison spent her professional life exploring the corrosive power of "Othering" those who we sense are different from ourselves. Her insights on the social construction of "Otherness" are worth pondering in our current era of scapegoating who or what is not just like us. Creating this and other forms of divisiveness within a country's citizenry is a poor substitute for authentic leadership that carries the largesse of wanting to unify while respecting differences.

Works Cited

Morrison, Toni. *Playing in the Dark: Whiteness and the Literary Imagination*. The William E. Massey Sr. Lectures in the History of American Civilization, 1990. Harvard UP, 1992.

---. *The Origin of Others*. The Charles Eliot Norton Lectures, 2016. Harvard UP, 2017.

Further Reading

Deardorf, Daniel. *The Other Within: The Genius of Deformity in Myth, Culture and Psyche*. White Cloud Press, 2004.

Johnson, Robert. *Owning Your Own Shadow: Understanding the Dark Side of the Psyche*. HarperSanFrancisco, 1991.

Ricoeur, Paul. *Oneself as Another*. Translated by Kathleen Blamy, U of Chicago P., 1992.

Slattery, Dennis Patrick. "Riting the Self as/and Other." *Riting Myth, Mythic Writing: Plotting Your Personal Story*. Fisher King Press, 2012, pp. 134-57.

21

WRITING AS A SPIRITUAL PRACTICE: A CONVERSATION WITH DR. MIKE PETROW

The following ideas were the spine for a conversation with my former Mythology student who is currently a pastor of a small church. I have chosen to leave them in the form that I initially created them.

August 21st, 2018

- Tell the story of your father bringing home a Scripto pen with four plastic ink cartridges. I sat on the arm of a chair by the front window in the living room and thought of what to write. I was 10 or 11. First, I copied out what I knew: The Our Father, Hail Mary and Glory Be. I loved the roteness of this exercise; I also loved the feel of the fountain pen's resistance across the paper as well as observing the purple letters forming across the page.
- Looking back over decades of writing, I realize that writing out the prayers was a form of spiritual meditation, one that involved the body, the emotions and memory. In my file drawers are many hundreds of pages of hand-written notes from books and drafts of books collected over the decades.

- After writing out the prayers, I was moved, incited to write a story about my two brothers and me on an adventure. I did and I enjoyed the experience immensely. I do not know what happened to these early writings. But I never forgot the joy I felt in creating a world that existed in only one field of reality: my imagination.

- Did my father see something in me that inspired him to bring this gift home for me? I don't know. Looking back at him now with the compassion I did not have then regarding his alcoholism, I do believe he did.

- In school even earlier, I loved to learn the alphabet and then to begin to print words out in block form on very grainy paper that easily showed the mulch from its processing from wood to paper. It was cheap paper that emanated a delicious aroma that I never tired of.

- When we had a spelling bee on Friday afternoons at Holy Cross School, I was one of two/three standing towards the end. Once in a while I would win. But the girls in the class were ace spellers so I usually went down before they did. But I loved spelling words. I could easily imagine them, see them in my mind, and simply said the letters out loud.

- I also served Mass at our Catholic church in Euclid, Ohio, east of Cleveland. It was located at Lake Shore Blvd and E. 200th Street. From there to the shores of Lake Erie was less than a ten-minute walk, five if I ran.

- I served Masses in the morning, sometimes the 6:15 Mass, which was very hard for those of us "chosen" for this early ritual because it made the school day very long. We had to memorize the mass in Latin, which I loved. I often did not always know what the words meant, but I loved to say them in another language. It was my introduction to learning a language other than English. It gave me a sense of power in knowing all the prayers and formal responses in the Mass. More importantly, perhaps, was the sound of Latin words, so smooth and silky to say. Their rhythms, when said aloud, were more pleasurable than English words, more friendly in a strange sort of way.

- I also think hearing the gospels for decades contributed to my interest and then love of stories themselves. It was a treat to hear the ancient narratives; I often tuned out the priest after that, when he launched into a homily around the story read for the Gospel of that day. I was content with the story itself. Often as he spoke, I would gaze around the walls of the church at the ceramic stations of the cross, which in their 14 "moments," depicted the now-familiar story of Christ's harrowing adventure, culminating in his burial. I knew that the story did not actually end there; a sequel was forthcoming.

I have kept journals for decades. Maybe I will ask my wife to destroy them when I die. I write every morning around a ritual. I sit with my journal and a cup of coffee after lighting a candle between 4:00-4:15. I have been getting up at 4 a.m. for about 30 years. I love the morning darkness, the quiet, the peace before the new day is fully born through the gates of dawn. What I wait for quietly each morning with my journal on a small portable wood desk with padding underneath, are the images and events from yesterday that wish to be recollected this morning. I write it down without ordering the events and the feelings that accompany them. It is often entries in chronological order, but not always. If a line of a poem shows up, I will write it down; maybe nothing happens after that. Sometimes I will write about what surprised me the day before or an incident that made me curious, something out of the ordinary.

Early morning is the best time to read poetry and to be aroused by a line that may seed a poem; this happens of its own accord. It is not quite automatic writing, but it is a writing announced, not demanded, summoned or even asked for. It just happens, prompted by energies or presences from somewhere, maybe deep inside but also from outside me. The poems have morphed into seven volumes of poetry, one just recently completed, co-authored with a former myth student, Craig Deininger.

I discovered that writing about the day before allows the divine goddess, Mnemosyne, mother of the nine Muses and patron of remembering, to enter my imagination. And what happens is that in writing, the day before, or two days back, begins to order or align itself with feelings, other memories, nuanced insights, to arouse in me patterns of awareness of a deeper consciousness. I think this situation begins the spiritual part of the practice. It feels at times like a form of therapy and of healing. The literal events of the previous day or days carry as cargo a deeper layer that, when invited, begins to appear, to take over, to run the vehicle without me. I am along for the ride and the opportunity to write. To ride *with it* summons me to write *about it*.

- If I am writing an article or a chapter or section of a book, it happens between 4:00-8:00 a.m. I have also learned when to quit; starting is the hardest part for many folks; quitting is hardest for me. As I ripen, my energy level dictates when to stop. Stopping is an art form requiring from me as much discipline as does beginning.

- Over the years I have enjoyed writing as a way of thinking about something. Writing is a way to discover what I don't know, what remains hidden until written down, which is so different from speaking. It is a magical imaginative moment, when ideas, as we say come to me, not as "breaking news" accompanied by harsh music, but more like the quiet emerging presence of the angel Gabriel when he visits the Blessed Virgin alone, in solitude, reading. Something often announces itself in these moments. Perhaps something virginal, something original, but certainly some notion that wants to be recognized and paid attention to.

- Reading certain subjects seems to promote writing ideas; reading and writing are twin sisters. They nourish one another. But the reading I am suggesting originates not from the ego's perspective; it happens from somewhere deeper, maybe from what psychologist C.G. Jung calls the Self, which is associated with or corresponds with the divine, with something transcendent and immanent at once.

- Both reading and writing further our own journey of individuation, of coming to an awareness of the complete self—shadows, shimmerings, values, prejudices, paradoxes, contradictions, perhaps adding up to a poetics of self. I think this process happens when we turn our attention to something other than ourselves, to contemplate it, which will always have analogies with and within our own creative spirit. Then something is invited in from an oblique angle, by indirection, rather than a frontal and formal confrontation.

- Dante is the one who revealed how, for example, his *Commedia* allowed him to participate, like God, in the creation of a world, a cosmos, a full and informed landscape design inspired by a sacred ordering principle. I don't believe he was suggesting he was God, but he was saying that in the creative process, somehow the entire world is recreated or reordered or set right in some important way. He carried the divine within and that one form of expressing that divinity within was to create; for him it took the form of writing. Another writer who develops this idea beautifully is Mircea Eliade, in his *Myth and Reality* volume; I paraphrase his thought below.

- To read, or reread, to write or rewrite, is to create oneself anew. These human actions have connections with what is divine in us, regardless of whether one finds a particular religion helpful in this quest or not. I think our natural wisdom is one form our divinity assumes; it invites access to what promotes wonder, questions, or concerns that put us into a larger orbit of awareness and understanding. For me that access happens most often through excess; I have to have overdone it, read too much, pondered in excess, have too many sources. Overload is the path to insight; this is a crucial element of my personal myth. I do not have 600 volumes in my private library; I have over 6000, many of them never read. See what I mean? Even unread, they have an effect on me in my work.

Here I list a few notions about writing from my book, *Riting Myth, Mythic Writing: Plotting Your Personal Story:*

- Writing is a form of discovery. Inherent in anything we wish to contemplate is an inner form that energizes and organizes the experience.

- Writing is a bearing witness to an event, a memory, a dream, a trauma, a movement of joy wherein some formed reality seeks voice. It may also be seeking solace.
- Writing allows me to break something down into edible parts so I can digest it, recycle it, spiral back to it, remember it, retrieve it and revision it anew.
- Writing brings shards of my personal myth into greater conscious presence and into a larger field of meaning through a form of rhetorical midwifery.
- I find it very beneficial, where ever I go, to carry with me a small spiral notebook and a pen that fits into my shirt pocket If the psyche knows you are ready and willing to receive ideas, notions, possibilities, then it will reschedule its route and deliver. I have many of these little notebooks on top of my file cabinet. They are filled with recommended movies, series, books, articles, web sites, a B&B in Austin, Texas, someone to contact in Dallas, and the like. If I do not slow down and write down these suggestions immediately, they will be gone in a matter of minutes. I need to fix them in place and decide later if they are worth pursuing. Sometimes ideas or notions for an entire article are birthed in this simple way. All the imagination requires most often is a nudge north or east. Writing it down sets the compass in motion.

I have made solitary retreats for decades. My first was as a high school senior at St. Joseph's High School in Cleveland, Ohio, in May of 1963. Next door to the school was an old diocesan retreat house used by the entire community. But when I entered it on Friday afternoon and emerged from it Sunday at noon, I knew I had been to another galaxy.

Not until June of 1971, when I finished my first year of high school teaching at Lorain Catholic High School in Lorain, Ohio, did Father Bill Snyder, a priest at the school, recommend I try Gethsemane Monastery in Trappist, Kentucky for a longer retreat. On my first retreat there, to which I rode my BMW motorcycle to heighten the adventure, I was introduced to the writings of Benedictine priest Thomas Merton, initially by his personal secretary, Brother Patrick Hart, who took me to Father Merton's grave beside the monastery wall. Over the next 20 years I made 10 retreats there. I had fully embraced the Western Monastic Tradition of the Catholic Church.

Years later, in 1998 and my first sabbatical from academe, when I was then teaching at Pacifica Graduate Institute in Carpinteria, California, and with the encouragement of my wife, I packed my Ford Ranger pickup truck and headed out on a 3.5 month pilgrimage to 12 monasteries and Zen Buddhist centers in the Western United States. I journaled religiously throughout the pilgrimage and, more than a year later, began to write from those notes a spiritual memoir, *Grace in the Desert: Awakening to the Gifts of Monastic Life*. Years later I revised and expanded that initial, much-shortened work into a more complete version, *A Pilgrimage Beyond Belief: Spiritual Journeys Through Christian and Buddhist Monasteries of the American West*. I think it may be the most important book I have yet written. In memoir form, it revealed to me ways in which the spiritual journey of writing is as profound as the outer pilgrimage to these spiritual centers—Buddhist, Carmelite, Franciscan, Benedictine, Dominican, as well as other lay retreat centers.

- To one of those monasteries, The Hermitage in Big Sur where I began my earlier pilgrimage, I return as often as possible for 5-day retreats. I think my love of the monastic life was given a huge injection when I studied for and became an Oblate at this Benedictine holy place some 11 years ago. The Oblate program rests on the belief that a lay person can, in his/her own way, serve the world through prayer, contemplation and service, as St. Benedict outlined it in his *Rules*. At one point in my life as a high school student, I entertained becoming a Marianist brother and intended to enroll at the University of Dayton; I ultimately chose another path. Perhaps better said, another path found and persuaded me otherwise.

- Becoming an Oblate within a monastery I love has satisfied my desire for monkhood. When I am there on silent retreat, I can fill half of a journal with meditative writing as I reflect on spiritual readings early in the morning in my monastic space. My practice there is to arrive at the chapel a half hour early before the service, sit quietly in the semi-darkness and write. I let what wants to be offered up to come in. I feel in these quiet peaceful moments, interrupted only by one of the brothers preparing the chapel for the service, like a scribe dutifully scratching in a journal what I am dictated. At other times I copy out a particular reading for that day from one of the Missals.

- This idea is so important. I don't ever ask: What do I write about? Instead, I sit quietly and something comes in, usually special delivery, a form of a monastic version of Fed-Ex, which I then obediently tattoo into my journal. Writing, the act of writing, promotes more ideas or insights, an image or a memory; all of these can be moments when a part of our personal myth is revealed to us for further contemplation; they are often moments of spiritual awakening in the slow and modest baking of an idea, an image or a revelation. I see these as gifts of annunciation, as Mary received as she quietly read in solitude, open to the visitation from the archangel Gabriel. These can be life-altering moments of a recommendation for another path to engage.

- They are also a way of healing, for I believe that when we write, we heal something in ourselves. We do not have to consciously know where we are broken for healing to begin.

- For those who wish to incorporate writing into their spiritual practice, I suggest Evelyn Underhill's fine title, *Practical Mysticism*. There she develops the idea that the poet and the mystic are cut from the same cloth.

- Also beneficial is Louise DeSalvo's *Writing as a Way of Healing*. Edward Whitmont's *The Alchemy of Healing* offers inviting areas to write within. My *Riting Myth, Mythic Writing.: Plotting Your Personal Story* is filled with prompts for meditation on a host of subjects. I took with me my notes and organized this book at the monastery I am discussing in this essay, after conducting personal myth writing retreats for years. My audience consists of folks who would like to use writing as a vehicle to explore deeper understandings of who they are. Other titles include Linda Leonard's *The Call to Create* and Rollo May's *The Courage to Create*. A more recent book which I was fortunate enough to co-author with Deborah Anne Quibell and Jennifer Leigh Selig is *Deep Creativity: Seven Ways to Spark Your Creative Spirit.* All of these titles will serve you as thoughtful guides for your writing and spiritual lives.

The popular mythologist, Joseph Campbell, put himself on the world cultural map in writing *The Hero with a Thousand Faces.* Worth reading. He reveals that the beckoning, or the call, which we all have delivered to us in one form or another, begins with hearing it, then heeding it, then submitting to it. What we hear and submit to is much bigger than ourselves; otherwise, it is not a summons but a reinforcement of who we already are. The titles above are all also relevant to the act of writing; one need not head out for the territory to be on one's personal journey; the acts of reading and writing can also deliver us to that mysterious terrain of contemplation that fosters a deepening awareness of ourselves in the more panoramic scheme of things. To this great adventure I congratulate you for undertaking.

Books Mentioned

Campbell, Joseph. *The Hero with a Thousand Faces.* Bollingen Series XVII. Third Edition. New World Library, 2008.

DeSalvo, Louise. *Writing as a Way of Healing: How Telling Our Stories Transforms Our Lives.* White Cloud Press, 2004.

Joe Fassler, editor. *Light the Dark: Writers on Creativity, Inspiration, and the Artistic Process.* Penguin Books, 2017.

Leonard, Linda Schierse. *The Call to Create: Celebrating Acts of Imagination.* Harmony Books, 2000.

May, Rollo. *The Courage to Create.* W.W. Norton, 1975.

Nelson, G. Lynn. *Writing and Being: Taking Back Our Lives Through the Power of Language.* LuraMedia, 1994

Slattery, Dennis Patrick. *A Pilgrimage Beyond Belief: Spiritual Journeys Through Christian and Buddhist Monasteries of the American West.* Angelico Press, 2017.

---. *Riting Myth, Mythic Writing: Plotting Your Personal Story.* Fisher King Press, 2012.

Whitmont, Edward C. *The Alchemy of Healing: Psyche and Soma.* North Atlantic Books, 1993.

22

A Sudden Scrape with Honesty[*]

People often say that we can't know when disaster, in the form of an illness, an accident, or a painful and heart-rending loss, will abrupt into our lives. These situations are all vulnerable to the mystery of life and the unforeseen that is part of our daily round. I think a worse condition would be that we *do know* when they are approaching, especially if there is little we can do about both their intention and their insistence.

But the same can be said about acts of kindness and, perhaps more to the point of this recollection, acts of honesty. We do not know when either an act of kindness or a display of honesty or courage will descend on us as a gift from a higher presence, nor how we will respond to such a surprising moment. We also cannot know when a situation will present itself that calls on us to assist another. So here is the story.

It was a day that began like any other when I headed to Das Rec in New Braunfels, Texas to swim laps and enjoy a hot shower. I felt good about getting back into the water after two weeks of travel where no pools were available. When I finished, showered, and headed out to my truck parked close to the entrance, a rare find for me, all seemed joyfully ordinary as I prepared to head home. I was already contemplating what needed to be done to the yard and the house and I looked forward to these simple yet fulfilling tasks.

---

[*] Published in the Opinion page of New Braunfels' *The Herald-Zeitung*" Thursday January 30th, 2020. A-4.

As I approached my truck, I noticed a man standing on the curb where some trees were planted. I assumed that he might be waiting for a ride to pick him up. I did not believe I knew him, but the friendly atmosphere at Das Rec encourages all of us to speak to one another and perhaps even discover a new friend in the mix. So I remarked that the weather was warm, making it easier for us who took showers inside to avoid getting a chill, or some such innocent observation.

He in turn asked me if the black Nissan truck we were now both close to was mine. I replied that it was and noticed as I walked toward the driver's door that there was a folded yellow piece of paper under the wiper blade. As I reached to remove it from the truck, the man told me he had written it because he had hit the front of my truck when he pulled into the parking space next to me. But then he continued: "I felt that leaving my name, telephone numbers and a note that I had hit your truck's front end was not good enough, so I decided to wait until whoever owns it came out so I could tell the person directly." I stood there amazed at what was unfolding before me through this man's admission—not a confession, really—but more akin to an observation that this event had happened and he postponed his day to report it.

My first response was gratitude; I thanked him for the effort he had made in writing the note, and then staying to meet whoever's vehicle had been damaged so he could tell them in person. This time *I* was that *them*. We then both shared how we had each, in the past, had our respective vehicles pinged, dented, scraped, or otherwise damaged by a desperado who immediately or clandestinely or both, drove off, leaving the wounds of their carelessness or recklessness or heedlessness there to be patched and paid for by the owner of the vehicle. Easier that way--not so messy. Less expensive. And not so honest.

But this man, who we both soon realized, lived on the same street as I but we had only spoken once before. So, we "knew" one another only in a very superficial, yet neighborly way. And the damage? Well, not terrible, that is to say, nothing that several hundred dollars at a collision shop off of I-35 could not remedy through restoration.

But that is not what was restored here. What was reinstalled for me was this generous and thoughtful individual who could have easily fled and parked somewhere else after the hit, with no one else the wiser. Instead, he chose to acknowledge what had happened in this brush with our two vehicles and wanted to remedy it through repair.

He asked me to take it to the body shop, get an estimate in writing and bring it to his home. It took a day or two, but I was able to have the estimate itemized and brought it to him a day or two later. The repair would cost $600.00 and would be done in the next three days. The repair shop kept its word and did excellent work.

Then, together, we drove in his vehicle, the one that had brushed with mine, to pick up my truck, now with a very professional face lift on its left front side. He paid the bill, we admired the expert repair, and we agreed to stay in touch. He drove off and I, with the repairs done to restore my truck to its newness, though eight years old, left the collision repair shop meditating on what had happened during this past week.

Now, months later, I continue to hold this incident and this man in my imagination as a gesture of honesty and courage to assist and guide me when I grow dark about the self-centeredness around me, or when I despair at times over the display by a few of some of our less-admirable human tendencies. This man had redeemed them and, in the process, I had been privileged, even singled out, to scrape against real honesty that was as refreshing and renewing as any scraping and repainting of my truck, which enjoyed its new front-end gleam. With his permission I now name him: Fred Faris, a beacon of integrity and a model for doing what is right. I wish all of you readers the same gesture of generosity and courage if you find yourself in the midst of a similar scrape with life. Having Fred as a neighbor is another gift that did not escape me.

23

Is All News "Breaking"?[*]

The news does not tell you how the seed is germinating in the ground, but it may tell you when the first sprout breaks through the surface.

~Walter Lippmann, *Public Opinion,* 147

In structure, format and perhaps intention, what is loosely referred to as "the news" or "the news of the day" has changed significantly from the days of Cronkite, Murrow, Rather, Reynolds, Jennings, and the most notable teams, McNeill-Lehrer News Hour and the Huntley-Brinkley report. I recently asked myself a few basic questions amidst the news-glutted world we seem to be mired in, whatever our personal or political preferences: What *is* the news and who makes that decision? Who is the audience for any news story? What in every news story is heightened so to be remembered and what is insisted or encouraged to be forgotten through what the particular story highlights and lowlights? What is a news story up to besides, or in addition to, the information it aims at deploying? Is its major intention to entertain more than it is to inform or indoctrinate? All of these questions are moving targets.

Choose any news show with or without a panel of commentators huddled around a table of donuts (never fruit). Of course, since this essay was originally written, individuals are Zoomed in from their living rooms, basements and kitchen tables as protection from the

[*] Published in the Opinion page of New Braunfels' *The Herald-Zeitung,* Thursday, January 9th, 2020. A-4.

Covid-19 virus. Zoom me in, Scotty! Each is a particular brand of spun information; its engines of production or reproduction are powered by a certain mythology. By that term I mean a particular bundle or passel of beliefs, values, feelings and even ideologies and philosophies that it sells with the same alacrity as the ads that break the news into menus of edible bites. Pose this question as you watch your favorite news show: what is the mythology filtering the information that promises to in-form me? Perhaps in answering this question, we note an observation by Brooke Gladstone, co-host of *On the Media* that might help. In her powerful and insightful series of ruminations in *The Trouble With Reality,* she suggests that we live in a time of electronic media where "the unknowing or unhinged can coalesce a vast number of like-minded souls into a force so powerful it can shift reality's prism or elect a president" (2). So, we have evolved within the news media and the technologies that promote them wherein there are islands of reality and often little shared beliefs.

She goes on to develop the above quote: "Part of the problem stems from the fact that facts, even a lot of facts, do not constitute reality. Reality is what forms after we filter, arrange, and prioritize those facts and marinate them in our values and traditions. Reality is personal" (2). Of course, today's "news" shows are populated with several commentators whose main task will be to reconstruct the facts of the story along mythopoetic lines, shaping and framing it to fit a point of view. A myth, I want to add here, is a point of view towards facts. Remember the clever detective, Joe Friday of *Dragnet* in the 1960s, whose mantra in questioning persons who might help solve a crime was: "The facts, ma'am, just the facts." His task was their interpretation by assembling them with other facts in order to see a pattern, a motive, a suspect. Today the news media does all of this for us.

A few years ago, as I watched one of my favorite news/group conversation channels, I asked myself: what is this story or shaped conversation asking/insisting that I remember, that I carry around with me like a portable shoulder bag *and* what stories or contents for discussion are asking/insisting that I forget, not notice, leave by the side of the road as irrelevant to the parts of the story I am coached to remember? I began to sense how "shaped" the news is (let us not forget it is a business), as well as who their audience is to be shaped at the same time. We are as audience shaped into the story being reported and discussed. Perhaps it is truer to say that we are *always* the story to be discussed.

Our attitudes are open for repair and rebuilding as much as our beliefs are that assist the attitude-shaping enterprise that is the news, breaking or not. Not only is the news politicized to fit a particular container, we too are politicized in watching and listening not just to the stories but to the order and arrangement in which they are conveyed. I will say this in a different way below.

The second question I posed to myself is not disconnected from the above. Regardless of the source of our news—magazines, newspapers, podcasts or other online sources, as well as one another—are we not only receiving in-form-ation, but also being re-shaped, re-formed and re-enforced by being so in-formed? For "news" informs and shapes how we know—a particular *way* or via of knowing, which may be in many instances more powerful than *what* we know. Moreover, the construction is not just limited to knowledge but more and more to how we are led *to feel* about what we know. News has become so feeling-toned in the contemporary world that it often supersedes the information itself. So is that the major enterprise now: to make me feel in a particular way towards what is being conveyed under the rubric "news"?

Earlier I used the word mythology, which includes but travels way beyond stories of ancient gods and heroes. Myths are more than that; indeed, they are consciousness-shaping and altering. Myths have the capacity and the power to shape our awareness through the kinds of beliefs they propose that incubate in us. Each news channel works off of a very precisely-delineated mythology to form the what/how of our perceptions of that increasingly slippery term, *reality*.

As to what we take in as news-worthy being either fallacious or valid—that depends on what mythology we care to feed most frequently and which we consciously or unconsciously choose to ignore, defile or starve to death. All news is sculpted, packaged and delivered both to construct a certain shaped reality while simultaneously either explicitly or overtly to debunk another version of that same news content. Pushed to the extreme, such a pattern of purpose can stretch out to invite in a totalitarian state.

Writing in 1941, the fiction writer and political analyst George Orwell, who gave us the literary classics *Animal Farm* and *1984*, expressed the following insight: "Totalitarianism's. . . control of thought is not only negative, but positive. It not only forbids you to express—even to *think*—certain thoughts but it dictates what you *shall* think, it creates an ideology for you, it tries to govern your emotional life as well as setting up a code of conduct" (*Orwell on Truth* 61).

A country's people must remain vigilant about the news that is presented as well as their own powers of discernment in parsing the news as true from the news as ideologically-torqued to shift your attitude and your felt sense of the worlds, not necessarily your knowledge-base.

To test the above, here's a dare: Once a week watch a news channel that you generally ignore or debunk for reasons you can easily enunciate, and see how their presentation of "the news" pushes the buttons that activate and irritate your more set ways of thinking and feeling. My guess is that you will feel viscerally the power of myth as well as how the news is most always emotionally-inflected and charged. I sense that you will get a rise out of this recognition! I've tried it and all my buttons lit up.

Works Cited

Gladstone, Brooke. *The Trouble with Reality: A Rumination on Moral Panic in Our Time.* Workman Publishing, 2017.

Lippmann, Walter. *Public Opinion: How People Decide; The Role of News, Propaganda and Manufactured Consent in Modern Democracy and Political Elections.* Adansonia P., 2018. Originally published in 1922.

Orwell, George. *Orwell on Truth.* Mariner Books, 2017.

Further Reading

Bok, Sissela. *Lying: Moral Choice in Public and Private Life.* Vintage, 1999.

Jacoby, Susan. *The Age of American Unreason in a Culture of Lies.* Vintage, 2018.

24

EXPLORING THOUGHTS
ON TYRANNY*

It does not happen with the frequency it used to that I impulse-buy a book in a bookstore, even one at an international airport that often carries both a surprising variety of classics as well as contemporary fiction and non-fiction. Perhaps the smallness of the book is what attracted me, but it had a very BIG title: *On Tyranny: Twenty Lessons from the Twentieth Century* by Timothy Snyder. Snyder is a well-known and acclaimed cultural historian. Two of his many other titles are *Black Earth: The Holocaust as History and Warning* and *Ukrainian History: Russian Policy and European Futures.*

"Tyranny" is a big word with many barbs shooting off of it. The word feels as big as the Titanic, so lumbering and unmanageable, but I wanted to see what Snyder had to say about its meaning and its presence in the world today; I bought it and read it on my flight home and subsequently. Each of the twenty lessons appears on its own page with a paragraph in bold beneath: some samples: 1) Do not obey in advance; 5) Remember professional ethics; 9) Be kind to our language; 12) Make eye contact and small talk; 15) Contribute to good causes. But # 10 caught and held my eye: Believe in truth. His first observation followed: "To abandon facts is to abandon freedom. If nothing is true, then no one can criticize power, because there is no basis on which to do so" (65).

---

* Published in the Opinion page of New Braunfels' *The Herald-Zeitung*'s on Thursday, March 5th, 2020. A-4.

From there he highlights four elements that burrow into the death of truth, according to Victor Klemperer, a scholar and historian who wrote diaries during the powerful and relentless rise of the Third Reich. His many works are considered reliable eye witnesses of that regime and others in Germany:

- "Open hostility to verifiable reality, which takes the form of presenting inventions and lies as if they were facts" (66). Confusion arises when the facts of events are continually hijacked by fabrications, which in turn breeds confusion as to what to believe. The truth begins to bleed out. The operative phrase in his quote is the very slippery "as-if."

- "Shamanistic incantation." "Endless repetition," according to Klemperer, "is designed to make the fictional plausible and the criminal desirable" (67). Nicknames, stereotyping individuals, referring to them as "lying" or "crooked" or "slimy" or "fake," repeated endlessly can give to any nonreflective people the sense that these illusions are the reality to embrace.

- "Magical Thinking, or the open embrace of contradiction" (67). Such occurs when people listen to and accept two realities that cannot exist at the same time, as with the presidential promise of "cutting taxes for everyone, eliminating national debt and increasing spending on both social policy and national defense." These promises undercut one another and cannot be made into a defensible belief. But one must grasp its illogic in order to see its impossibility. George Orwell coined a term for this kind of dizzying version of reality: "doublespeak" became the strategy in *Ninety Eighty-Four* to create alternate forms of existence by assaulting any form of shared reality that was not constructed by those scrambling to achieve or who had attained power. The Power Elite becomes, then, the entity to defeat.

- "Misplaced faith": (68). Here one attempts to self-deify, to make one seem a god who can perform the impossible, alone. "I alone can solve it," or "I am your voice," or "I am the committee." What is attacked on this level of truth-killing are "the small truths of our individual discernment and experience" (68). We are no longer encouraged to believe in our own validity or those that our experiences teach us. We gladly relinquish them to the authorities, and with it, our own agency as citizens who have rendered ourselves impotent. We become one with the anonymous masses.

- While the entirety of Snyder's book reveals that this same game plan has been used repeatedly in the past, I found it helpful and not a little frightening to see it anew within the historical context he outlines. And like a slow-moving ocean liner, sometimes its motion is hardly detectable. History shows us NOW what was THEN. Snyder's insights insist that we pay vigilant attention to the web of contexts being spun around us so we do not relinquish our freedom to the force of innuendo.

Work Cited

Snyder, Timothy. *On Tyranny: Twenty Lessons from the Twentieth Century.* Tim Duggan Books, 2017.

Further Reading

Anderson, Kurt. *Fantasyland: How America Went Haywire. A 500 Year History.* Random House, 2017.

Hedges, Chris. *Empire of Illusion: The End of Literacy and the Triumph of Spectacle.* Nation Books, 2009.

Orwell, George. *1984.* Harcourt, Brace and Company, 1949.

Slater, Lauren. *Lying: A Metaphorical Memoir.* Penguin Books, 2001.

25

CONVERSATIONS IN A DIGITAL AGE: THE CORE OF CIVILIZATION*

Now here is a book title that will appeal to a large audience and one I have just completed reading: *Reclaiming Conversation: The Power of Talk in a Digital Age* by Sherry Turkle. Published in 2016, her research and discoveries are astonishing and perhaps even more relevant today. Working with young people in schools, she has measured how texting, emails, and other technological means of communication have lowered the level of empathy one feels for another and others. The smart phone, she believes, has altered not only behavior with one another, but threatened the prospect of intimacy itself. Smart phones sit at the dinner table and restaurants like an additional guest, face-up, ready to be pounced on when it rings or buzzes; fear of boredom is the major player among 18-24 years old, Turkle has discovered, so the computer or cell phone is the new Linus security blanket promising instant escape from solitude, being alone or feeling bored, isolated, and left out. It is also the default corridor to escape conversation.

Her research discloses that the technology we lionize is also the technology that can silence us, especially in shutting down conversation, either on the phone or face-to-face. Her subjects tell her that they would rather text someone than talk to the person directly.

* Originally published as "Civilized Conversation in a Digital Age." Published in the Opinion page of New Braunfels' *The Herald-Zeitung*, September 22nd, 2019. 4-A.

Fear of not getting it right is the main reason presented for avoiding situations where conversation with another is encouraged; one might say something and get it wrong. There is no time to edit or to control the communication when it is "live." Turkle uses the image that far from conversing more, we connect more; connection overrides conversing. Consequently, we can find ourselves in a "technological cockpit," isolated from any ideas, notions, feelings or beliefs that do not agree with our own. Most of us realize that conversation, real conversing, throws one into ambiguity, into a place where ideas take on their own life, and are not so controllable and sometimes not so agreeable to everyone engaged in an exchange. But the trade-off, if one is willing to be open, can also lead to new insights, ways of thinking and fresh contexts not considered before. Yes, learning is risky business. Many would rather remain cocooned in their tiny incubator, completely enraptured by the technology, than risk being wrong or wronged.

She insists that there is hope in retrieving conversation, which is directly linked to civilization. Civilization brings up its beginning word, "civility." Bullying, Turkle suggests, especially on-line bullying, may be experiencing such an alarming acceleration because one does not have to witness the other person's reactions, their feelings, or the trauma incited when bullying is isolated through technology. Technology is a powerful buffer against human experience. Empathy is erased or sharply curtailed by technology because the other person persecuted is not present in an embodied way as an individual, nor can their emotions be seen, much less experienced by the bully.

Conversation moves in a counter direction: it promotes intimacy and uncertainty; in conversation one is not fighting to be right or to win, but to understand the point of view of another and one's own, more fully. Conversation can actually encourage compassion for the other and for one's self. "Face-to-face conversation unfolds slowly. It teaches patience. We attend to tone and nuance. When we communicate on our digital devices, we learn different habits.... We dumb down our communications, even on the most important matters. We may also become accustomed to a life of constant interruption" (35) that allows only the briefest of sound-bytes. Contemplating an idea or a feeling in-depth becomes almost impossible. The context opposes such duration.

"Conversation needs duration and durability." Real conversation, not passing information back and forth, can serve as "a crucible for discovery" (37). Ideas "come from speaking." What matters most in conversation is risk-taking. "The thrill of 'risky talk' comes from being in the presence of and in close connection to your listener" (38). One relinquishes control in order to allow ideas to have their own way, to see where they lead and what connections might be stirred in the crucible of time and duration, not in the pauses between constant interruption.

Turkle's research reveals that "the average adult checks his/her phone every 6.5 minutes; teenagers send an average of 100 texts per day. Eighty percent sleep with their phones and will check them when they roll over during a night's sleep; 44% never unplug from their devices" (42). These figures may be much higher now. The behavior is both compulsive and addictive. Instead of spurning interruptions, we then tend to welcome them to keep the wolf of boredom on the other side of the door. Stillness is eliminated; solitude turns to loneliness and terrifies; we multi-task and concentrate on something for only a few minutes or even seconds. Our lives can easily become scattered and so full of busyness that at the end of the day we are left with little to reflect on; in fact, reflection seems a lost art, which is a terrible forfeiture because it is first cousin to conversation. The end result is a shallow and incomplete sense of who we even are as a person.

Perhaps more than a little of the brutality we see today in human interactions from the personal to the political realms directly mirrors how technology is insisting on training us how to relate to one another in both skimpier and more aggressive ways. Lee Worth Bailey suggests in his insightful study that "*Human desires are always involved in technologies*" (*Enchantments* 21). Are we losing sight of where one ends and the other begins or has the line disappeared?

Nonetheless, Turkle remains hopeful; she believes we can reclaim conversation, and with it an earlier form of intimacy, community and basic human respect for one another's point of view, without necessarily acquiescing to it. Listening is often more than enough, wherein the other feels heard. Shrill attacks on what another thinks or believes reduces our humanness and with it, civilization itself is dealt a wounding blow. Coercion towards uniformity goes a long way to erasing the treasures inherent in differences.

True conversation is one of those rare win-win human delights. Not winners and losers.

For Reflection:

- How has your cell phone changed your behavior?
- Are you happy with the changes?
- Does your cell phone control you or do you exert control over it?
- If you were driving to a destination and half-way there realized you had left your cell phone at home, would you turn around to retrieve it?
- When you meet friends in a social setting, is your cell phone visible and checked as you enjoy one another's company?
- How much effort is needed NOT to answer your phone when you are with others?
- What in the article above hit home the most?

Works Cited

Bailey, Lee Worth. *The Enchantments of Technology.* U of Illinois P., 2005.

Turkle, Sherry. *Reclaiming Conversation: The Power of Talk in a Digital Age.* Penguin Books, 2015.

Further Reading

Carr, Nicholas. *The Shallows: What the Internet is Doing to Our Brains.* W.W. Norton, 2010.

Jackson, Maggie. *Distracted: The Erosion of Attention and the Coming Dark Age.* Prometheus Books, 2018.

Jacobs, Jane. *Dark Age Ahead.* Random House, 2004.

26

WHEN MY TIME COMES[*]

We may ask ourselves early in life: How should I live? Later, as we ripen into ourselves and expand our awareness of the inner and outer worlds we migrate between, our question may shift to "How have I lived?" Aging, like illness, may include a constantly shifting perspective in reflective moments in order to answer both questions.

Diane Rehm's new book, *When My Time Comes: Conversations About Whether Those Who are Dying Should Have the Right to Determine When Life Should End,* brings us at least two additional areas to contemplate: "How shall I die?" and "Under what circumstances?" Perhaps we add a third: "Who will make the final decision: I who am dying from a terminal illness or others?"

Many of you may know Rehm from her 37-year career hosting *The Diane Rehm Show* and who now offers a podcast, *On My Mind.* From her own experiences with her mother's death, which was very painful, to her husband of many decades who also suffered the pains of terminal illness the last months of his life, she has become a strong advocate for a growing movement, Medical Assistance in Dying (MAID). Her book of twenty-three interviews embraces a wide range of voices who are for and who resist such "interference" in the natural death of a terminally ill patient who has been judged to have less than six months to live and who wishes to preserve their own agency surrounding when they die and under what conditions.

---

[*] Originally published as "When My Time Comes." Published in the Opinion page of New Braunfels' *The Herald-Zeitung,* March 26th, 2020. A-4.

Currently in the United States there are nine states which have passed laws allowing medically-assisted dying; those who support such a choice are careful, generally, not to use the phrase "medically assisted suicide" because proponents do not see it as assisting suicide but assisting dying. I bring this up because even the language of the debate is under constant scrutiny and discussion, if not heated legal, ethical, medical and religious perspectives.

Doctors, palliative care physicians, priests, ministers, spouses and loved ones of those who suffered intensely at the end of their lives, directors of spiritual care and hospice programs, professors of medicine, terminally ill patients, attorneys, state legislators and Rehm's own grandson, who interviews his grandmother, are among those included in her survey of opinions. Rehm is a superb interviewer with special gifts and skills which she brought to over three million people who regularly listened to her broadcasts. I found the interviews both engaging, disturbing, persuasive and thought-provoking on a subject that in the United States is in many quarters still taboo to converse about. Rehm's intention is to begin/continue conversations, not drub the reader with her favored position.

Some of the key questions posed include:

- What terms or conditions should be present when it is decided—and by whom? —to keep an individual alive?
- To what end?
- Who is one terminally ill and suffering benefiting or comforting by being kept alive beyond their own desire to die?
- Should the religious or moral beliefs of a doctor or medical professional in charge of a patient be the final arbitrator of one who is suffering intensely while dying?
- Should the wishes of the patient be held foremost such that they can exercise control over their own deaths?
- What is one's definition of a good death? Rehm asked every person interviewed to respond to this question, including herself.
- What does one want when near the end of life?
- Should the "End of Life Option Act" be decided by legislators in each state?

- Who should have a voice in such a challenging topic and what weight should their opinion hold?
- Is medical aid in dying in fact a form of cloaked suicide?
- What does it mean, finally, to "die a natural death" with the aid of pain-relieving drugs?

I found reading this book challenging my own beliefs. I ended completely supporting Rehm's desire to deepen authentic conversations about our options for dying, which is part of the natural cycle of life. How much and how often we should intervene in that process depends largely on how we define "natural cycle." Whatever our definition, it will most likely keep the tension in place between allowing one to choose their death and medical technology's desire to keep one alive, even when doing so robs personal agency from the patient in the last stage of their existence.

Work Cited

Rehm, Diane. *When My Time Comes: Conversations About Whether Those Who Are Dying Should Have the Right to Determine When Life Should End.* Foreword by John Grisham. Alfred A. Knopf, 2020.

Further Reading

Becker, Ernest. *The Denial of Death.* MacMillan, 1973.
Brown, Norman O. *Life Against Death: The Psychoanalytical Meaning of History.* Random House, 1959.
Chodron, Pema. *The Places That Scare You: A Guide to Fearlessness in Difficult Times.* Shambhala Publications, 2002.
Gawande, Atul. *Being Mortal: Medicine and What Matters in Life.* Henry Holt and Company, 2014.
Hine, Virginia. *Last Letter to the Pebble People.* Foreword by Elisabeth Kübler-Ross. Unity Press, 1979.
Jacoby, Susan. *Never Say Die: The Myth and Marketing of the New Old Age.* Pantheon Books, 2011.
Mitford, Jessica. *The American Way of Death Revisited.* Vintage Books, 1998.

Sawin, Leslie, et. al, editors. *Jung and Aging: Possibilities and Potentials for the Second Half of Life*. Spring Journal Books, 2014.

Smink, Edward M. *The Soul of Caregiving: A Caregiver's Guide to Healing and Transformation*. Wise Media Group, 2018.

Smith, Rodney. *Lessons from the Dying*. Wisdom Publications, 1998.

Yates, Jenny, editor. *Jung on Death and Immortality*. Princeton UP, 1999.

27

The Texas Coalition to Abolish the Death Penalty[*]

On Saturday, February 29th 2020, I attended my first conference sponsored by the Texas Coalition to Abolish the Death Penalty (TCADP) at the Whitley Theological Center of the Oblate School of Theology in San Antonio, Texas. It was titled "2020 Vision for Texas: A Leap Towards Justice." I admit that I have believed for years that the death penalty as a general rule revealed a failure of imagination by those in the criminal justice system to deal with certainly horrific crimes, but I was convinced there were alternatives available for those charged with committing the crime. When my friend Dr. Roger Barnes, chair of the Sociology Department at the University of the Incarnate Word, invited me I thought I should attend to hear what members of the TCADP had to say about the death penalty's presence and effectiveness in Texas, their rationale for wanting to abolish it, and the history of such an ineffectual deterrent to violent crimes that currently warrants such a punishment.

Ms. Kristen Houle Cuellar, executive of the organization, opened with an elegant welcome and a report on current statistics regarding death penalty cases in Texas and nationally. About 125 people were in attendance. The day's menu was too abundant to describe, so I will

---

[*] Forthcoming in the "Another View" section of *The San Antonio Express-News.*

focus on the morning panel discussion moderated by Dr. Barnes and including Mr. Sam Millsap, a trial lawyer, who "was elected Bexar County District Attorney in 1982 and served in that office until 1987." Also a panelist was current Bexar County District Attorney, Joe Gonzales, who has served the county for the past 13 months.

Lasting about 80 minutes, the panel was packed with an almost dizzying array of facts, histories of individual cases, and reminiscences by Mr. Millsap from his term as District Attorney. The question posed to the two panelists by Dr. Barnes kept the conversation moving briskly. Their responses touched on legal, moral and psychological areas of concern. They included as well what still needs to be accomplished by all concerned citizens to abolish the death penalty in Texas.

Here is a sample of the kinds of questions posed to the two attorneys: 1) "How did you/do you determine when to seek death in a murder case?" 3) Do you/did you feel pressure from the community to seek the death penalty?" 6) "Is the death penalty a human rights violation?" 7) "What were you taught about the death penalty in law school?" 9) "Does the death penalty act as a deterrent to murder?"

In response to question #1, Mr. Gonzales said that the degree of a horrific offense would influence his decision to seek the death penalty. He added, however, that of 28 cases currently pending as possible instances for the death penalty, only 1 is moving forward in that category. In responding to question #3, Mr. Millsap noted that, yes, he had felt pressure in the mid-1980s when he served as District Attorney. In response to question #6, both attorneys affirmed that in their mind the death penalty is a human rights violation. Furthermore, neither men believed they had received much instruction on the death penalty in law school. Only when Mr. Millsap was asked to teach a course on the death penalty at St. Mary's University Law School did he realize how scant was his information on the subject. Both men answered "no" to question #9, that surrounding the death penalty there is no conclusive data that reveals the death penalty deters murderers.

Mr. Millsap then compared regions of New England and the Southern United States. The former had not had death penalties for many years, citing Maine in particular, who abolished the death penalty in 1887. Southern states do have the death penalty and have executed 1241 inmates stretching back to 1976. Yet in the northeast, homicide rates are lower than in southern states. In Texas specifically, there have been 569 executions since 1976.

Both men believe that if we had "true life" sentences without parole, the case for ending the death penalty, perhaps nationally, would be much stronger. Colorado, both men pointed out, has a bill currently on the Governor's desk, and he has announced his plans to sign it, which would make Colorado the 22nd state to abolish the death penalty. The trend seems to be moving in that direction for additional reasons: the discovery now of the number of individuals who were wrongly convicted, as well as the crippling financial impact for housing inmates on death row. They both offered that Texas is shifting in public sentiment away from capital punishment but may not yet be ready to overturn it.

I end with a few items from a helpful list of "Facts About the Death Penalty" that accompanied the program for the day. I've retained the bold formatting from the original document.

- New death penalties in Texas have **decreased significantly** since peaking in 1999.
- In 2019, new death sentences remained in the **single digits** for the fifth year in a row.
- Over the last five years, **more than 70% of death sentences** have been imposed on people of color.
- **Only four counties** in Texas (Harris, Smith, Tarrant and Walker) have imposed more than one death sentence in the last five years.
- The state of Texas has executed **569 people** since 1982, accounting for more than one-third of the 1,515 executions nationwide since 1977.
- The state of Texas has **executed two people to date this year** and is scheduled to carry out **seven more executions** in the first few months of 2020.
- In Texas, the cost of an average death penalty case is **nearly three times higher** than imprisoning someone for life without the possibility of parole.
- **21 states** have abandoned the death penalty through legislation or judicial decisions. Governors in four other states have imposed moratoria on executions.

- **142 countries** have abolished the death penalty in law or practice. In 2018, the top five executing countries were China, Iran, Saudi Arabia, Vietnam, and Iraq.

Options to putting inmates to death, perhaps incorrectly, are certainly available if the cultural imagination is willing to consider them. Reflecting back on the part of the conference I was able to attend, I realize how much more aware I had become in just a few hours. I do not believe that my time at this first meeting with such a dedicated group will be my last.

Left to right: Mr. Sam Millsap, Mr. Joe Gonzales and Dr. Roger Barnes.
Photo courtesy of Dr. Karin Barnes

28

CURIOSITY SKILLED THE CAT[*]

All human beings, by nature, desire to know.

~Aristotle, qtd. in *Curiosity*, 22

A book I had bought years ago, brought home, shelved and soon forgot about, whispered to me the other morning that it was ready to be read. I obliged. It is called simply *Curiosity* by Alberto Manguel. I purchased it for the obvious reason that I was curious about what curiosity is, beyond my current understanding.

The author, from Buenos Aires, tells a story early on of walking home from yet another new school as a youth. He had fallen into a set routine but had grown bored taking the same way home every day, so, diverted from his well-grooved pattern by the powers of curiosity, he took a side street and soon became lost. He could only offer in retrospect when asked, that he did not know why he diverged from his familiar path that day except to say "I wanted to experience something new, to follow whatever clues I might find to mysteries not yet apparent" (9), which then led him on an adventure that was less frightening than it was energizing because it exacted a feeling of wonder in him. In fact, it was such an adventure, that when he eventually "turned a corner and found myself on familiar ground" and spotted his own house, "it felt like a disappointment" (12).

[*] Originally published in the Opinion page of New Braunfels' *The Herald Zeitung,* February 27th, 2020. A-4.

He also learned at a young age how reading could provide him untold divergences from the familiar. He realized what many of us have discovered: that reading always seems to include the acts of remembering, revising and renewing what we may have thought was already settled and fixed-in-place in our lives for the duration. This process of reading also insists we take on what is new and find a place for it in the household of the familiar.

As I continued to read his stimulating adventure, I began to consider that curiosity's constant companion is consciousness itself; a certain degree of intensity is necessary to even arouse my wonder about something. Becoming curious, wondering about something or someone, asking why, who, and what is perhaps one of the most valued human gifts we hold and can continually cultivate in ourselves. When I need a refresher course on curiosity, I visit our younger son's family and always strike up a conversation with my older granddaughter, Eleanor, age 7; she is a wonder-filled child who wants to know why about everything. Her imaginative life is at full throttle right now and her love of learning to read is a consequence of such abundance. Being around her always renews my awakening to be curious, especially when I watch her play or struggle over a sentence's words and their meaning as she learns to read. Curiosity to know drives her pursuits in all their forms.

Not wealth but wonder seems to be a signal of true abundance; said another way, wonder is one of our delightful forms of wealth. In his introduction, Manguel believes "we imagine in order to exist, and we are curious in order to feed our imaginative desires" (3).

But then he moves to a discussion that intrigued me even more: "Imagination as an essential creative activity, develops with practice, not through successes . . . but through failures." His reasoning may surprise some: "failures force us, if we are curious enough, to try again, to pursue a different tact that may lead to new failures" (9). My own failures have always pushed me to question what I had been assuming and to revisit with a bit more humility what I wish to achieve.

Our culture has as one of its bumper stickers: "Failure is not an option." I wonder where this idea came from, an idea that is not only unrealistic but harmful. Of course, learning to fail better runs against this popular and misleading bromide. Failing can actually free us from the fantasies that gather around success in order to imagine more deeply and, depending on the trajectory of our curiosity, lead to unforeseen surprises and new ways of knowing what once seemed so familiar and ordinary.

But to the other side, a question: are there people, things, situations, conditions or beliefs that we should not only *not* be curious about, but also not question? To leave these arenas at the doorstep of "It is what it is"? Maybe. I think, however, that whatever exists we have a right to be curious about and to question; the danger of not doing so can lull us into accepting what, finally, attests to be untrue, or worse, uninteresting and boring. It may be wiser to fail in our curiosity than to yield too complacently to what lacks sufficient veracity.

To know a great deal of information is not to be wiser; it may just make one fuller. Ask people, right now in their lives, or earlier, when they were full of the zest of wonder, what they are/were curious about. Their answers you might find extremely curious. Being curious carries with it its own elegant form of vitality for life.

Work Cited

Manguel, Alberto. *Curiosity*. Yale UP, 2015.

Further Reading

Alighieri, Dante. *The Divine Comedy*. Translated by Allen Mandelbaum, Alfred A. Knopf, 1995.

Bohm, David and F. David Peat. *Science, Order, and Creativity*. 2nd edition, Routledge, 1987.

Damasio, Antonio. *The Feeling of What Happens: Body and Emotion in the Making of Consciousness*. Harcourt, Inc., 1999.

Isaacson, Walter. *Leonardo Da Vinci*. Simon and Schuster, 2017.

Jung, C.G. *Memories, Dreams, Reflections*. Edited by Aniela Jaffee, Random House, 1963.

McAdams, Dan P. *The Stories We Live By: Personal Myths and the Making of the Self*. Guilford Press, 1993.

Melville, Herman. *Moby-Dick; Or, The Whale*. Edited by Hershel Parker and Harrison Hayford, W.W. Norton, 2002, pp. 1-427.

Quibell, Deborah Anne, Jennifer Leigh Selig and Dennis Patrick
    Slattery. *Deep Creativity: Seven Ways to Spark Your Creative Spirit.*
    Foreword by Thomas Moore. Shambhala Publications, 2019.
Slattery, Dennis Patrick. *From War to Wonder: Recovering Your Personal
    Myth Through Homer's* Odyssey. Mandorla Books, 2019.
Steindel-Rast, Brother David. *Gratefulness, The Heart of Prayer: An
    Approach to Life in Fullness.* Paulist Press, 1984.
Taylor, Daniel. *The Healing Power of Stories: Creating Yourself Through the
    Stories of Your Life.* Doubleday, 1996.

29

An Attitude of Gratitude*

And that trust in the Giver is the crucial point where faith and gratefulness meet.

~Brother David Steindl-Rast, *Gratefulness,* 105

Finding a medicine to arrest the Covid-19 virus (CV) in the body of those who test positive for it, as well as a vaccine that will prevent it, are both indispensable. Time becomes more urgent; the sooner the better.

In the meantime, something else strikes me as important in this global challenge: the attitude we each take up in our daily lives, which has to do with how we think about and respond to the CV's threat. The Swiss psychiatrist and cultural mythologist, C.G. Jung (1875-1961), whose writings stretch across more than 20 volumes, offered an extensive description of the power and importance of the attitudes we carry into any daily situation, whatever its level of complexity and force.

Jung suggests that on its most basic level, an attitude is "a state of readiness" (*CW* 6, par. 687). The attitude we deploy to any life situation will shape how we think about it, imagine it, and respond to it. Attitudes are as important to our way of being as our breathing.

As the CV unfolds in terrifying numbers globally and in our own nation, we hear or read of individuals or groups who live "as if" there

---

* Originally published in the Opinion page of New Braunfels' *The Herald-Zeitung,* April 16th, 2020. A-4.

is no virus or no systemic threat to them, even as it continues globally to infect over four million people and kill tens of thousands of others. My estimates here may be woefully low.

Jung advises that we cannot perceive either the outer world or the inner world without a guiding attitude to help us navigate both terrains. I am learning that an attitude contours what we each select and claim as relevant as well as what we are inclined to leave along the side of the road as immaterial, untrue, unimportant or simply non-existent.

Our habitual attitudes tend to gravitate towards what is familiar or has proven to be security-promoting and meaning-making, such that when a significant new reality enters our world, especially something as violently infectious as the CV, we might tend to force it into the habitual attitude that sustains us in order to lessen its destructive nature and even trivialize its presence. When a habitual attitude will not budge, then any new reality must be persuaded or coerced into fitting into its mold or simply be discarded.

Of course, another possible option is that the individual or the collective shifts its attitude in order to face head-on and apprehend more of the new content's reality. The startling discovery here is that the attitude(s) that we cultivate figure largely into what reality we are capable of—and willing to—absorb. A shift in attitude is also nothing less than a transformation of consciousness. Such a conversion means that one's manner of selecting a certain set of perceptions, feelings, and thoughts that comprise what one has decided to be conscious of, what is most important to pay attention to, and to reflect or meditate on, fundamentally determines what reality one lives, and perhaps dies, by.

Something as massive as the current coronovirus can push us to the edge of our comfort zone, and perhaps in some cases, shove us forcefully into a new attitudinal zone of awareness. Some may find themselves breaking the mold of an old attitude which has outlived its reassuring qualities and no longer serves the dominant myth that guides them. I ask myself with each news cycle and readings on this mysterious, vicious and ubiquitous entity:

- What is my own attitude towards coronovirus?
- How am I responding to it and what is that or those responses serving?
- What am I willing to give up to contribute to arresting its spread?

- Can I sacrifice parts of my life in order to serve a greater good?
- Can I suffer all the restraints put on my life now until I am told it is safe to resume many activities I enjoy later?

C.G. Jung observed that depending on our attitude, we can be swallowed up by the way we think and respond to any life situation (*CW* 6, par. 690), or we can be liberated by a shift in attitude, especially one that guides us to further self-understanding.

In the midst of our growing differences as to how to respond to the current pandemic, one attitude is clear that we all share: the deep gratitude for all public servants in many professions whose attitude of serving others, even while it has risked or cost them their own lives, is unconquerable. Their generous attitude towards those infected are models of consciousness we might all try to emulate.

Works Cited

Jung, C.G. *Psychological Types*. Vol. 6. *The Collected Works of C.G. Jung*. Sir Herbert Read, Michael Fordham, et. al, editors, a revision by R.F.C. Hull of the translation by J. G. Baynes. Princeton UP, 1990.

Steindel-Rast, Brother David. *Gratefulness, The Heart of Prayer: An Approach to Life in Fullness*. Paulist Press, 1984.

Further Reading

Chodron, Pema. *Welcoming the Unwelcome: Wholehearted Living in a Brokenhearted World*. Shambhala Publications, 2019.

---. *Taking the Leap: Freeing Ourselves from Old Habits and Fears*. Shambhala Publications, 2010.

Fulghum, Robert. *From Beginning to End: The Rituals of Our Lives*. Ivy Books, 1995.

Johnson, Robert A. *Inner Work: Using Dreams and Active Imagination for Personal Growth*. HarperSanFrancisco, 1966.

Slattery, Dennis Patrick: *A Pilgrimage Beyond Belief: Spiritual Journeys Through Christian and Buddhist Monasteries of the American West.* Revised and expanded edition. Angelico Press, 2017.

---. *Day-to-Day Dante: Exploring Personal Myth Through the Divine Comedy.* iUniverse, 2011.

30

THE WAR THAT CAME TO CAMPUS: REMEMBERING KENT STATE, A HALF-CENTURY LATER[*]

Like untold numbers of other events in our country and around the world, the Commemoration Weekend on May 4th, 2020 organized to remember the horrific killing and wounding of Kent State University students, was reluctantly cancelled. I had planned to attend. In the absence of that ability because of the Covid-19 pandemic, I want to tell my story of that fatal experience.

As a graduate student in Comparative Literature spring quarter in 1970, I arrived on campus for an afternoon class about 90 minutes after the shootings. My former creative writing teacher and good friend, Barbara Child, told me later that when she heard the first M-1 rifle fire, she looked at her watch: 12:24 pm. Here is what I remember.

I was teaching eleven students in a Special Education program in the Ravenna School District for my second year. I was given permission by the school's principal to attend a graduate class on Monday afternoons so I could complete the degree that summer. When I arrived on campus, parked and entered Satterfield Hall, the English Department building, I knew something was wrong; no students or faculty were in the halls. Usually crowded with both groups

[*] Originally published in the "Another View" section of *The San Antonio Express-News*, May 2nd, 2020, as "From Afar, Recalling the Horror of Kent State." A-11.

busily changing classes, it was now quiet and deserted. Disoriented, and as I questioned my own reality at that moment, an English Department faculty member, Professor Marovitz, ran down the hall toward me. When I saw that his trajectory was to scoot right past me, I stopped him and demanded: "Where is everyone?!" His terrified response—"They are killing our students"—before he broke free from me and ran out a side door.

Dumbfounded, I headed out the same door and up a gentle rise of grass leading to the rim of the Commons area. There, in complete silence, were some 2000 people lining the rim of what was called "Blanket Hill," which sloped down to the Commons area and to the famous Liberty Bell that was rung when Kent State athletes won a game. All were simply standing, frozen in place; no one was talking. I approached clusters of five to six Ohio National Guardsmen in a circle but, facing out, with their bayoneted rifles pointing to the sky; when I slowed my pace and looked into their grim faces, I saw terror in their eyes. What had happened? I did not know then that just a short time earlier, they had indiscriminately opened fire on the masses of students and faculty who had gathered to demonstrate against both the escalating Vietnam War and the recent invasion into Cambodia by the United States.

I was to learn subsequently that students had been killed and wounded. The four killed were Allison Krause, Sandra Scheuer, William Knox Schroeder and Jeffrey Miller, whose names are part of a memorial on campus that it took 20 years in court battles to finally erect. They, as well as nine wounded students, had already been taken off campus. I had entered the drama and the trauma at a lull, a pause, a moment of paralysis and disbelief, that had stunned everyone into silence; but it was not to last much longer. It was now approximately 2:20 pm.

As we all looked, transfixed, down from the rim of the bowl to the Commons area, we could see the numerous police officers in riot gear begin to assemble in pairs, then move resolutely up Blanket Hill towards the top of the rim where we stood. In an instant, 2000 people scattered—into buildings, behind cars, across and behind other buildings—fearing another burst of bullets aimed at them. As the chaos intensified, a car with a loudspeaker boomed from the Commons area: "By order of Ohio Governor James Rhodes, this campus is officially closed." We were told that all inhabitants must leave the campus within hours. With that, thousands of the 20,000 students enrolled that quarter began to gather their belongings; everyone living in dorms hastily packed and began exiting the campus.

Stunned and frightened, I rushed back to my car and drove home to a house we rented in the city of Kent. A decree went out shortly in the city that anyone could leave, but if one did not have a driver's license with a current Kent address on it, or could not show proof of living there, they would not be allowed to re-enter the city. The closest conditions to a fully-militarized police state was immediately put in place and lasted for at least two weeks, as I recall. My wife and I had Kent addresses on our licenses, so we were able to continue to teach in our respective schools in Ravenna, some 15 miles east, but we were stopped each time by police or National Guards at the city limits to show proof of residency. Small tanks and unmarked black cars patrolled the streets around the clock.

The numerous events so carefully planned, some of which I had tickets to attend the ceremonies on May 4th, 2020 will happen in virtual space, but I have little interest in attending. I did, however, attend the services held on May 3rd at the Unitarian Universalist Church in Kent on Zoom. But coming to the campus physically cannot be substituted. To walk the Commons area where the guards and police gathered, to see the pockmarks in the Liberty Bell from several rifle bullets fired at random into the crowds of students, and to pay homage to the memorial in memory of the dead, cannot be experienced from afar.

While none of us can be there, on site, we can remember that fateful day, May 4th, which also falls on a Monday this year, when the war in Vietnam came on to campus and changed a part of the collective psyche of our country permanently. The wounding must be remembered every year without any yielding to the pressures in some quarters that say it is time to stop remembering and to move on. To what? is never expressed.

Further Reading

Backderf, Derf. *Kent State: Four Dead in Ohio.* Abrams Comic Arts.
    Forthcoming.

Child, Barbara. *Memories of a Vietnam Vet: What I Have Remembered and
    What He Could Not Forget.* Chiron Publications, 2019.

Esterhas, Joe and Michael Roberts. *Thirteen Seconds: Confrontation at
    Kent State.* Gray & Company Publishers, 1970.

LePore, Jill. "Blood on the Green: Kent State and the War that Never
    Ended." *The New Yorker,* May 4, 2020, pp. 70-75.

Michener, James A. *Kent State: What Happened and Why.* Random
    House, 1971.

See https://www.kent.edu/may4kentstate50

About The Author

Dennis Patrick Slattery, Ph.D., has been teaching for fifty-two years, the last twenty-six in the Mythological Studies Program at Pacifica Graduate Institute in Carpinteria, California. He is the author, co-author, editor, or co-editor of thirty volumes, including seven volumes of poetry: *Casting the Shadows: Selected Poems; Just Below the Water Line: Selected Poems; Twisted Sky: Selected Poems; The Beauty Between Words: Selected Poems* with Chris Paris; *Feathered Ladder: Selected Poems* with Brian Landis; *Road, Frame Window: A Poetics of Seeing. Selected Poetry* with Timothy J. Donohue and Donald Carlson; and *Leaves from the World Tree: Selected Poems* with Craig Deininger. He has co-authored one novel, *Simon's Crossing,* with Charles Asher. Other titles include *The Idiot: Dostoevsky's Fantastic Prince. A Phenomenological Approach; The Wounded Body: Remembering the Markings of Flesh; Creases in Culture: Essays Toward a Poetics of Depth;* and *Bridge Work: Essays on Mythology, Literature and Psychology.* With Lionel Corbett he has co-edited and contributed to *Psychology at the Threshold* and *Depth Psychology: Meditations in the Field;* with Glen Slater he has co-edited and contributed to *Varieties of Mythic Experience: Essays on Religion, Psyche and Culture;* and *A Limbo of Shards: Essays on Memory, Myth and Metaphor.* His more recent books include *Our Daily Breach: Exploring Your Personal Myth through Herman Melville's* Moby-Dick; *Day-to-Day Dante: Exploring Personal Myth Through* The Divine Comedy; and *Riting Myth, Mythic Writing: Plotting Your Personal Story.* With Jennifer Leigh Selig, he has coedited and contributed to *Re-Ensouling Education: Essays on the Importance of the Humanities in Schooling the Soul,* and *Reimagining Education: Essays on Reviving the Soul of Learning.* With Deborah Anne Quibell and Jennifer Leigh Selig he has co-authored an award-winning book, *Deep Creativity: Seven Ways to Spark Your Creative Spirit;* with Evans Lansing Smith he has co-edited *Correspondence: 1927-1987* on the letters of Joseph Campbell. He has also authored over 200 essays and reviews in books, magazines, newspapers, and online journals.

He offers "riting" retreats in the United States and Europe on exploring one's personal myth through the works of Joseph Campbell and C.G. Jung's *The Red Book.*

For recreation he takes classes painting mythic themes in both water color and acrylic. He also enjoys riding his Harley-Davidson motorcycle with his two sons, Matt and Steve, through the Hill Country roads of Texas.

Made in the USA
Monee, IL
03 August 2020